James Stewart Polshek

Context and Responsibility

James Stewart Polshek
Context and Responsibility

Buildings and Projects
1957-1987

Introductory Essays by
Helen Searing and Gwendolyn Wright

RIZZOLI
NEW YORK

On the front: 500 Park Tower, 1980 (photo ©
Timothy Hursley)
On the back: Teijin Applied Textile Science
Center, 1964 (photo © Kawasumi Architectural
Photographic Office)

First published in the United States of America
in 1988 by
Rizzoli International Publications, Inc.
597 Fifth Avenue, New York, NY 10017

Copyright © 1988 James Stewart Polshek

Library of Congress Cataloging-in-Publication Data
Polshek, James Stewart.
   James Stewart Polshek.

   Bibliography: p. 254
   1. Polshek, James Stewart. 2. Architects—
United States—Biography. 3. Architecture,
Modern—20th century—United States.
4. Architecture—United States. I. Title.
NA737.P55A2   1987   720'.92'4   87-45545
ISBN 0-8478-0876-9
ISBN 0-8478-0877-7 (pbk.)

Designed by Abigail Sturges
Set in type by Rainsford Type, Ridgefield, CT
Printed and bound in Japan

For
Ellyn, Peter, and Jenny

Contents

BUILDINGS AND PROJECTS

First number refers to in-text description; second number indicates where work may be found in illustrated section.

Acknowledgments This book is a distillation of thirty years of work as an architect and an educator. Its immediate genesis was an exhibition of a selection of our work for the Eidgenossische Technische Hochschule (ETH) in Zurich, entitled "Context and Responsibility."

The book could not have been written without the buildings and projects, and these would not exist without the 265 clients spanning thirty years. Their diversity is a reflection of the wide variety of projects the firm likes to undertake. Their unity has lain in their loyalty and intelligence, which has been a continuous source of inspiration.

Even with the assistance of my exceptional partners and associates, nothing could have come to fruition without the many other people who have worked in the office during these years and in all capacities—as designers, managers, and support staff. All those who have participated in the office at any given time join our "nuclear family," and when they leave, they simply become a part of our extended family. I also want to acknowledge and thank the dozens of structural and mechanical engineers, the many other consultants who deal with light and sight and sound, and the managers of the construction process who have been so much a part of making our drawings come alive.

There are a few people who have been directly instrumental in helping me with both the exhibition and the book whom I wish to thank specifically: Professor Herbert Kramel believed in my work and invited me to exhibit at the Eidgenossische Technische Hochschule, beginning the process that led to this book. Anne Seel, my assistant during 1985 and 1986, contributed significantly to the refinement and research for both exhibit and book. Alessandra Latour provided her remarkable organizational skills and assisted with the graphic design and text of the exhibit and the book. Without her continuous high spirits and exemplary energy, this project would still be on the "boards." Anne Boxall and Catherine Snodgrass have kept the processes in constant motion, producing and reproducing an ever-changing manuscript. I want to especially thank Leslie Thomas who stepped in at the very end and helped pull this complicated undertaking together. Abigail Sturges's graphic design and editorial advice were extremely helpful. Todd Schliemann, one of my principal design associates, played an important role in overseeing the development of new drawings. I owe a special debt of gratitude to Professor Helen Searing, the Alice Pratt Brown Professor of Art History at Smith College, for her trenchant editorial advice and her encouragement. I also want to thank Professor Gwendolyn Wright, Associate Professor at the Graduate School of Architecture, Planning, and Preservation at Columbia University, for sharing her editorial talents during the early stages of the manuscript. I wish to express my particular thanks to Stephanie Salomon of Rizzoli for patiently coping with an architect's prose. My partner, Joseph Fleischer, demonstrated his usual patience during the long period of research and production, and his excellent memory and editorial comments were tremendously helpful. Finally, I want to thank my wife, Ellyn Polshek, for applying her editorial skills, legal logic, and artistic sensitivity to the entire book. Without her precise intellect and persistence, I could not have succeeded in this effort.

Foreword

The true importance of architecture lies in its ability to solve human problems, not stylistic ones. A building is too permanent and too influential on public life and private comfort to be created primarily as "public art." Modern abstractions or nostalgic borrowings from the past cannot themselves generate ideas for structures of lasting value. Only buildings that serve broader social, political, or cultural purposes can achieve this.

Although the search for an ideal synthesis of tectonic and aesthetic principles will always prevail, there now exist conditions that are modifying the way architecture is taught and practiced. Limited financial resources for buildings, increased regulation by public authorities, diminished availability of craftsmen, and the exponential rise in construction litigation make it difficult for the architect to achieve a truly humanizing architecture. However, if he yields to these difficulties rather than adapting them to a larger vision, the architect will gradually lose the opportunity to perpetuate the civilizing ideals of society through architecture. He will become instead a decorator of neutral structures that are the physical representation of a society in decline. This has already taken place to a certain extent and has led to the current cynicism about the possibilities of the future. While the first half of this century was essentially characterized by optimism, the last half, beginning with the invention and use of nuclear weapons, has been marked by a publicly expressed pessimism. Although architecture necessarily depends upon the past, it is a profession of the future. My belief in this future has led me to try to create an architecture that can truly ameliorate human problems and thereby reinforce the heroic and optimistic aspects of the art of building. At the core of the search for a moral and ethical basis for practice lies the basic opposition of architecture's psychological and political dimensions—nature versus reason.

The psychological dimension of architecture is private. It involves the application of the ordering rules of geometry to the perception of form and space, and an understanding of the interconnected relationships of anticipation, experience, and memory. Anticipation requires the use of imagination. Experience cannot exist without realization. And memory imposes the need to integrate the experience with all that went before—the reinforcement and broadening of the anticipatory impulse.

The political dimension is public. It concerns the profession of architecture, the laws of building, social attitudes about place, and the relationships of money, power, and architecture. It also concerns the relationships of people to buildings—as users and observers.

In order to understand how the practice of architecture can incorporate the ideals of education and political action it is necessary to define the word *profession*. For this I rely upon the definition that Abraham Flexner gave over sixty years ago in defining the profession of medicine (Walter P. Metzger, "What is a Profession?" Seminar Reports: *Professionalism and Humane Values*, vol. 3 [New York: Program of General Education in the Humanities, Columbia University], pp. 1–3). There are six points, and they are as follows: first, the occupation has to possess and draw upon a store of knowledge that is more than ordinarily complex. Second, the occupation must secure a theoretical grasp of the phenomena with which it deals. A profession, in Flexner's view, is necessarily an intellectual enterprise. Third, the qualifying occupation must apply its theoretical and complex knowledge to the practical solution of human and social problems. Fourth, an occupation, to qualify as a profession, has to strive to add to and improve its stock of knowledge. Fifth, a profession must pass on what it knows to novice generations. Last, an occupation, to qualify as a profession, should be imbued with an altruistic spirit. Its members must perform fiduciary duties for the client and do charitable works for the needy public. Without elaborating on this last requirement, Flexner implies that all employments ruled by the quest for profit, rather than the itch for service, will not qualify as a profession.

If one measures the current practice of architecture against these definitions, one can conclude only that our undertakings should be the embodiment of synthesis and the opposite of fragmentation. Synthesis is consistent with the tenets of Modernism: optimism and belief in the humanistic uses of technology, and rationalism. Modernism also implies a belief in economic progress, ideal social orders, and the standardization of knowledge and production. All of these ideals are as real and accessible today as they were over sixty years ago.

Buildings, by their external monumental forms, spatial configurations, and surface iconography make public "statements" that express an architect's personal style. Buildings can also reinforce the positive aspects of human behavior and thus act as cultural and social stabilizers. They do this by the ways in which they condition behavior, that is, by helping to make "connections" between people and a variety of disparate visual stimuli and spaces. These connections lie beyond style—essentially altruistic and external. There are two types of connections which I characterize as the "private" and the "public." The private areas are concerned with the building itself and are spatial and tectonic. They determine the relationship between plan, section, and elevation. These, in turn, influence the quality of transition from street to lobby to vertical circulation to corridor to room—from public realm to private place. Also in this private category lie the connections of materials and structures that combine to become the details of the work. These details predict and validate the integrity of architecture as well as provide delight for both user and observer.

The second category of connections are the public ones. They determine the quality of the building's contribution to the urban environment and they govern the perceptions of the casual passerby, interested observer, and the user. These urbanistic connections, in turn, fall into two groups. The first has to do with the building's physical relationship to its contextual infrastructure of streets, sewer, electricity and water supply systems, and to the volumetric formation of its surroundings. The second group concerns the iconographic aspect of the building with respect to its public details and surface characteristics and its wall openings and profiles—in short, its visual relationship to its urban neighbors or its natural setting. These public connections are subsumed within the political dimension of architecture. Ultimately, the psychological and political dimensions converge. The place of convergence is the context, and the strategy of resolution is the building.

The projects presented here are described first in prose form, arranged chronologically in four phases so as to connect them to the social attitudes and political realities of their times. The first of these phases is an abbreviated autobiography telling how I came to be an architect. The second, third, and fourth phases deal with the evolution of the office, and in chronological order explain briefly the works that were undertaken. Each project is identified by a prose description and a small photograph that refers the reader to the detailed graphics of the projects located in the section entitled Context and Responsibility. Here, selected works are presented in eight generic contextual categories intended to show that the ability to create an architecture that can contribute to the solution of social and environmental problems is achievable. They are Urban Design, Preservation, Reinforcement, Reparation, Conservation, Completion, Creation and Interior Design. Each contextual category is introduced by an explanation of its strategic application to appropriate design problems. Each introduction is accompanied by images of four historic buildings that are significant precedents. It is important to note that no building project is so taxonomically "pure" that it fits neatly into any one category. I have placed

them according to what I believe are their dominant formative characteristics, anticipating that the reader will make his or her own connections among the various categories.

Finally, I hope I have produced a book that is more than a collection of photographs, but rather an affirmation of the idealistic proposition that it is possible to practice architecture in the second half of the twentieth century in an ethically and socially responsible manner.

JAMES STEWART POLSHEK

10

James Stewart Polshek as Form-Giver

Helen Searing

James Stewart Polshek's gifts as an architect are many and various. He is a rational problem solver, a sensitive restorer and amplifier of existing buildings, and a skillful organizer of volumes and surfaces and movement through space to satisfy interdependent but often divergent functional, technical, and social demands. Polshek is also an architect deeply responsive to form. While the work of his firm, James Stewart Polshek and Partners, may strike one most immediately by its sheer professional competence, lengthier encounters disclose a subtle manipulation of space, light, color, and materials to create a range of sensual effects that consistently, if cautiously, captivate.

Readers acquainted with Polshek's passionate fulminations against style may find heretical the suggestion that he is a form-giver, since one usually associates that term with creators of a manifestly personal style often achieved at the expense of fundamental pragmatic demands. But it is precisely because Polshek in his polemics relegates formal issues to a subordinate position that it is necessary for others to insist on the strong formal dimensions of his architecture. A designer continually aware of form in the world around him and greatly concerned with form-making in his own work, as Polshek is, does not inevitably pursue style for its own sake, a stance Polshek deplores. In any case, Polshek's architecture resists stylistic labeling, which may account for its otherwise inexplicable absence from trendy compendia on late Modern and Post-Modern architecture. Rather, the unifying characteristics must be sought in the larger approach of the firm to design, an approach that encourages an openness to many different forms—contemporary and traditional, Western and non-Western—and a willingness to assimilate and incorporate those forms when architecturally appropriate.

Intimately bound up with the firm's approach to design is the recognition that the major task and greatest challenge for today's architect is to mend the torn and tattered fabric of our cities and suburbs, to reknit what has been rent asunder by time, greed, and misguided notions of architecture and urbanism. To preserve and enhance the culturally viable artifact, to replace or remedy the visually or technically unsound one, and to respect the desirability of continuity while acknowledging the need for change are some of Polshek's most pressing and admirable goals.

Polshek has forged these goals through experiences that lie beyond as well as immediately within his professional training and practice. He and his wife, Ellyn, are avid travelers who enjoy exploring a wide variety of urban places and natural landscapes. Their exposure to

markedly contrasting cultural and architectural milieus, first during their residence in Denmark, and then in Japan, has reinforced an innate antipathy to ethnocentrism. In addition, Polshek's fifteen-year tenure as dean of the Graduate School of Architecture, Planning and Preservation at Columbia University has had a profound impact on his theory and practice of design. Contact with architecture students, so often at the cutting edge in their acquaintance with new ideas and their enthusiasm for innovative figures, kept him abreast of vanguard strategies, while his responsibility for the preservation program served to reaffirm his appreciation of craftsmanship and historic architecture, whether vernacular or monumental. Polshek was instrumental in establishing at Columbia University the Temple Hoyne Buell Center for the Study of American Architecture, and the motives generating his own work are perhaps best summarized by the theme of the Center's inaugural symposium, held in 1982: "Innovation and Tradition in American Architecture." Note that it is *and*, not *or*, and be aware that by *American* Polshek does not understand an exclusively Anglo-European synthesis.

This responsiveness to sources from diverse periods and places distinguishes Polshek from the typical form-giver in thrall to a single monolithic vision to be imposed on the world. Moreover, the unobtrusive absorption and transcendence of these sources in the making of an architecture contemporary in image and technique differentiates him from those whose borrowings, whether pure or eclectic, harmonious or dissonant, are deliberately flaunted. The visual, tactile, and kinesthetic experience of many of the firm's buildings may evoke historical associations, but identification of references is not a prerequisite to enjoyment. If the floating planes, chromatic palette, and hard-edged geometries of the headquarters of the AMRO bank bring intimations of De Stijl to the cognoscenti, the space will be no less psychologically resonant to the spectator innocent of the European avant-garde. In any event, the Dutch group never worked with the gleamingly sumptuous materials so in evidence here; the refinement of detail bears comparison, rather, with the work of Ludwig Mies van der Rohe or, more appropriately in this particular case, such followers as Gordon Bunshaft. More to the point, the final result is pure Polshek: the black-and-white walls have no antecedents, and lend to the dignified public space an exuberance that can be appreciated by all who enter it.

A very different set of enthusiasms—and requirements—governed the design of Washington Court. The Modernist insistence on frank expression of program has yielded a rhythmically rich composition that in its striking symmetry and its abstract shapes is indebted to Italian Rationalism, while in scale, color, and texture simultaneously respects the neighboring buildings of Greenwich Village. The deep reveals and shallow projections allow light to modulate and sculpt the exterior facades and enhance the complex's agreement with its nineteenth-century surroundings, whereas the sparer elevations facing the court evoke relevant European housing experiments of the 1920s that signaled stylistic innovation. The model for the spatially complex, light-filled duplexes was no doubt Le Corbusier's basic dwelling unit, the beloved *object-type* of the maisonette, in which vertical release and spatial interpenetration compensate for the restricted horizontal measurements.

Although there has been a demonstrable, and to this writer welcome, evolution toward inclusiveness and allusion in Polshek's work, he has not been a Jimmy-come-lately jumper onto the bandwagon of historical reference—unlike some principals in firms once considered bastions of corporate Modernism. Undoubtedly, his experience as one of the foremost restorers of historic buildings, including those of the American Renaissance, attuned him to respect early in his practice the visual values of the past. Furthermore, while retaining the social ideals that he absorbed during his training according to Bauhaus doctrines, Polshek soon moved away from the prescriptive formal straitjacket of orthodox Modern architecture and its self-referential narcissism, which has had such devastating effects on our cities. A turning point may have been in 1969, when he designed Twin Parks East, a publicly supported housing project. Working with the archetypal Modernist format of free-standing tower and slab set upon a plaza, Polshek dared to humanize the dwelling units by employing banding in contrasting colors to recall an earlier generation of apartment houses erected in the Bronx during the more ingratiating Art Deco era. At this date, the use of such non-structural polychromy for decorative effects was new, as was the contextual impulse that prompted it.

For insight into the dual processes of development and continuity in the Polshek practice, it is useful to compare Twin Parks with Liberty House, the residential tower recently completed in Battery Park City. In both housing projects, Polshek has used standardized components for budgetary reasons, inflected parts of the building to dramatize site relationships, and applied striking polychromatic cladding. But in Liberty House, the repetitive regularity of the fenestration has been mitigated through surface patterns, created by various materials as well as colors, that organize the elevation in a way comparable to that of the Beaux-Arts skyscraper. A playfulness that comes only with mastery emerges here as well, seen to particular effect in the streamlined cylindrical

crown that is directly indebted in its forms to the Modern, and Moderne, of the 1920s and 1930s. However the wit at work in Polshek's design is urbane, not frivolous, and thus consummately in keeping with the Manhattan setting of Liberty House.

Polshek's first major commissions, for Teijin Limited, reflect the Brutalist current that was dominant when he commenced independent practice. The *béton brut* that gave the movement its name is very much in evidence, and the combination of this material with coarsely laid brick pays homage to the hero of that moment, Le Corbusier. In keeping with Polshek's attitude toward allusion, the Corbusian references are not gratuitous; in a country where this architect's influence was then paramount, they constitute a palimpsest of Brutalist gestures that have extended to the work of such Japanese admirers of the Swiss-born master as Kunio Mayekawa, Kenzo Tange, and Kiyonori Kikutake. There are also references to the traditional samurai castles of Japan, which in the Applied Research Center may be glimpsed in the shapes of the canopies and in the stone base. Another graceful, but smaller-scale, merger of East and West, looking to a different Japanese type, the tea house, is the Donovan Pool Pavilion, where modern planning and structural solutions are informed with a comforting sense of older rituals.

In these early buildings, Polshek was not obliged to respect the architectural context, although the pool pavilion demanded sympathetic attention to the natural surroundings. The firm has continued to design free-standing buildings set on relatively open sites, but the challenge of adding to existing structures or inserting new ones into a dense urban matrix, increasingly the fare of architects today, seems to call forth Polshek's most discriminating talents. Such commissions impose restraints, but they also yield design clues and have stimulated Polshek to greater inventiveness, resulting in more complex and visually appealing works.

As a contextualist, Polshek is not content merely to replicate features of the extant surroundings, a method common today among some practitioners. His commitment to the use of modern materials and techniques of construction, and his ability to work within economic and legal constraints, would make that course unlikely. He prefers to foster an interchange between past and present, and his way of accomplishing this has grown more supple and personal over time. Initially, as a number of his peers were doing, he stressed the opposition of the new to the old, making if not a collision at least a contrast between them. Recently he has followed a more conciliatory procedure. The development can be traced in a comparison between the executed additions to the Glenfield Middle School in Montclair, New Jersey, and the project for the Metropolitan Park Tower in New York City.

At Montclair, the new and existing portions, although adeptly joined in relation to circulation and grouping of functions, are pitted against one another in other regards, and the original Neo-Georgian sections are definitely the losers. The block containing the acoustically remarkable theater is aligned with the existing school, but where the two would connect, a rotated line of circulation is introduced. The planetarium and the deck are organized along the new axis, while the library is the point of mediation between old and new paths. The aggressively contemporary detailing and the materials of the additions make no concession to the original building, but instead comment on its lack of distinction. This tactic represents a particular moment in contemporary architectural practice; thus Romaldo Giurgola, a member of the jury that in 1981 awarded the project a citation from *Progressive Architecture*, praised Polshek precisely because "He separates quite clearly the new event from the old one, and uses the old one as a backdrop" (*Progressive Architecture*, January, 1981, p. 132).

The project for Metropolitan Park Tower, to be erected adjacent to the Metropolitan Club, of 1894, is much more immediately sympathetic to the work to which it will be joined, undoubtedly because that work, by the firm of McKim, Mead & White, is of incomparably finer quality. The materials, the scale and detailing of the fenestration, and the articulation of the elevation, decorously respect McKim's American Renaissance design; that clash of two incompatible vocabularies seen in the Glenfield School, which some might find invigorating but others disconcerting, has been exchanged for a more harmonious coexistence between old and new. Furthermore, since the Metropolitan Club is now surrounded by taller buildings considerably larger in scale, Polshek's addition will restore to the building in its altered setting at Fifth Avenue and 60th Street the importance and authority it initially possessed.

Metropolitan Park Tower similarly serves as perfect foil, because the tasks are so comparable, to 500 Park Tower, Polshek's addition to the former World Headquarters of the Pepsi-Cola Company, erected in 1958–59 to the designs of Gordon Bunshaft, senior partner in the New York office of Skidmore, Owings & Merrill. The original buildings in each case are remarkably alike in size, and each represents the classic statement of its designer's architectural loyalties. The wide range of Polshek's abilities is confirmed in his responses to the two

commissions. It was probably more difficult to find a satisfactory solution to expanding Bunshaft's little gem, because its distilled simplicity offered fewer opportunities for dialogue, than it was to add on to McKim's building, the eclectic, ornamental vocabulary of which offers so many clues for compatible detailing. The difficulty was compounded by the necessity for reorganizing the interiors of the Skidmore, Owings & Merrill work without sacrificing the integrity of the exterior. Polshek managed to subdivide the universal spaces characteristic of corporate architecture in the 1950s and 1960s into offices that now offer greater privacy and spatial interest. For 500 Park Tower itself, Polshek's earlier allegiance to the sources of Skidmore, Owings & Merrill's late Modernism stood him in good stead. He has enriched the reductive refinement of the mature Miesians with echoes of Constructivism and De Stijl, and in the granite-clad portion reinforced the prior claims of the typical New York-style skyscraper. The residential portion's recessed fenestration is played off against the adjacent strip windows, set flush in the surface in a manner that once epitomized the International Style. 500 Park Avenue also stirs memories of that earlier masterpiece of European Modernism as interpreted by George Howe (chairman when Polshek attended the Yale University Architecture School) and William Lescaze for the American financial community: Philadelphia's PSFS building of 1930–32. There are clear parallels in the way the volumes interpenetrate and in the treatment of the fenestration. The PSFS building comes to mind again when one enters the AMRO Bank.

In standing back—restoring existing buildings, where he must subordinate his own personality to that of the previous architects, and designing additions, where he must tackle the stressful job of welding old and new—Polshek stands out in his profession. Some of its members have rivaled film stars in media attention by seeming to cater to the same inexhaustible popular appetite for new images and fashions that are consumed as rapidly, and with as much ultimate satisfaction, as cotton candy. Within the last decade he and his associates have found their own voice as an architectural firm, and it is a powerful one that has begun to gain a hearing among the lay public, by giving equal weight to the three commandments that have defined the architect's mandate since antiquity: *Utilitas, Firmitas, Venustas*, that is, a functional plan, a firm structure, and visual delight. To this he has added the Modernist ideal of the architect as servant of the diverse needs of the community, but he has given this ideal a new and more authentic dimension. As a form-giver he has maintained his commitment to the spirit of Modernism while freeing himself from the alienating potential of its legacy.

The Challenge of Constraints

Gwendolyn Wright

The architecture of James Stewart Polshek evokes both the restrained elegance of a specifically Modernist idiom and the multiple associations of urban design. Such multiplicities overlap at many levels. Polshek's buildings often defy exact dating, yet they are incontrovertibly contemporary; although they look authentically new, we feel they have been just where they are for a long time—indeed, some of the recent structures could even pass for major renovations, as if the core had long belonged on the site. These buildings also live both a public and a private existence. Designed in response to diverse pressures, of which formal ideas are only one element, they convey layers of meaning to different groups: speaking to the historian about precedents, to other architects about the complexity of the design process, they can still engage the public in a discussion about simple visual pleasure and important continuities. In a better world, all architecture would engage in such exchanges, rather than presuming that one narrow discourse is indeed universal.

This approach to architecture consequently suggests a different way to think about history and historical responsibility in both the professional and the public realm. First, at a formal level, the work testifies to the ongoing validity of Modernism—that is, to a renewed Modernism that can now engage the metropolis and the local past, embracing cultural complexity. This is not the austerity, the rational purity of form, the disdain for American architecture and culture, that have long characterized the International Style in this country.

Here is a version that still holds to the formal principles and moral concerns of the early European movement, while coexisting comfortably with, and even drawing from, the varieties of forms and human associations in today's cities.

This Modernism goes beyond artificial purity in another way as well, by openly acknowledging the actual process of design in the world—the inevitable give-and-take, the spirit of adaptation and argument that constantly affects the transition from initial idea to final building. Too often the history of architecture is taught as if this sequence involves outside forces hacking away at pure design, eroding content. Polshek builds out of engagement with the multiple constraints imposed not only by the client, but by history, the city, and interested non-user parties. He seems to work at his best in the difficult progression from concept to realization. Content, we realize, emerges from the interaction of formal concepts and social realities. Of course, the process is seldom easy or direct; yet the architect's perceived prerogative

to have the last say about what is appropriate, symbolic, or simply attractive does not have to mean foreclosing such debate.

The result, in fact, can give architecture an enhanced public significance. It no longer seems feasible to say that design can solve major social problems, but good design and sensible methods can help resolve smaller difficulties. The State Bar Association Headquarters in Albany, New York, to take one example, demonstrates that an architect can respond to preservationist groups, satisfy his client's needs, and still explore purely formal problems. When local community groups and the New York Landmarks Preservation Commission suggested that various "historic" details be added to Washington Court, Polshek, in response, reemphasized the more abstract ways—color, materials, proportion, building line, detailing—in which the complex responded to the varied settings, both commercial and residential, of a Greenwich Village avenue. Such an attitude toward constraints is certainly welcome. The demands the world poses for any architect—conflicting interest groups, governmental and community agencies, even a difficult budget or a historic site—can seem either inappropriate impositions or exciting challenges.

As a result, the work also represents an important statement about history in the public sphere, specifically about the role of contemporary architecture. We recognize here the ongoing quality of history: it is not possible to stop time in an effort to retain the aura of a bygone era, as some people would like, but neither can innovators choose to ignore immediate local circumstances and sentiments. Polshek's work consistently shows great respect for the past—for the ordinary buildings of American cities, as well as for architectural and cultural monuments here and abroad. Yet we never sense a timid reserve with restorations or new creations, never a denial of the passage of time history involves. Even purely preservationist projects, such as the restoration of Carnegie Hall, can still incorporate innovative elements without betraying the responsibility to respect buildings that people have come to love. In part through efforts to recapture the excitement of an original design scheme, in part by abstracting qualities such as musical culture or religious ritual, and in part simply by addressing new functions and uses, architecture inevitably introduces change. One discovers new details, technological improvements, even new spaces introduced in boldly fitting ways. Restoration, renovation, and new design can all celebrate cultural history.

Polshek's own adherence to the Modernism of the 1920s

has itself been modified by history, and he clearly recognizes the transformation—in himself and in the culture. To use this vocabulary today is as much a statement about history as using a classical pediment would be. In either case, it is the formal principles and symbolic associations that matter and deserve to be maintained. We have become too sensitive to differences—conflicting traditions and preferences, inequities and inappropriateness—to insist that any form is universally valid without modification. Each project is therefore necessarily distinct, in terms of design and the process leading up to that design. The particularities of each client and each site, as well as the architect's own personal evolution, necessitate such eclecticism. One, nonetheless, discerns an indisputably individual signature throughout Polshek's work: a fascination with technology that enhances comfort, a sensitivity to connections (both architectural and natural) beyond the building, a formal predilection toward horizontality, proportional systems that generate plans, and always a tactile love of materials (most often the Modernist catalog of sleek aluminum, glass, and steel, but also the elegance of marble or the rough texture of brick). Distinctions emerge in part from the logic of the firm's evolution over time, in part from the specific concerns of each problem.

There is much in this characterization that would seem to associate James Stewart Polshek with Post-Modernism. But, in fact, the association is superficial. Polshek does not take the historical break separating us from early Modernism as a license to do whatever he pleases. He still insists on the legitimacy of architecture's social responsibility. The issues are less grandiose than they once were, the aesthetic less self-consciously pure, but the conviction remains that architecture can affect how people think and how they live. Environmental planning is one example of this attitude, appropriately tied to a very contemporary social concern. The Quinco Mental Health Center, for example, is not simply well sited; its design derived in part from the effort to preserve a natural setting from destruction while providing patients with a calming vista of woods and water. Even more striking is the North County Resource Recovery Center, where one finds a synthesis of architecture and landscape that cuts across history, from the seventeenth-century formal garden to the twentieth-century viewing platform over the waste-recycling plant.

This stance can even lead to a quality all too rare in contemporary design, but desperately needed in modern cities: architectural restraint. The tower at 500 Park Avenue deferentially bows to the smaller Pepsi-Cola Build-

ing (an elegant 1960 structure by Gordon Bunshaft of Skidmore, Owings & Merrill, only eleven stories high), not simply in a single gesture, but rather through an elegant minuet of textures, setbacks, details, and composition that enhances the smaller building. Detroit's Stroh River Place invigorates the moribund industrial structures on the site, notably Albert Kahn's 1929 Parke-Davis factory, by highlighting their simple tectonic qualities, then linking the complex to the city and its riverfront—both techniques noticeably more humane than the nearby Renaissance Center.

Perhaps the Brooklyn Museum project best testifies to this spirit of a new Modernism, which ties architecture into an existing urban pattern even as it innovates. Collaboration, of course, involved not only the museum staff, but also another architect, Arata Isozaki. Their joint scheme connects the museum to the adjacent Botanical Garden and the city streets through a system of shifted axes and terraces. This extension outward, together with the sensitive restoration of McKim's monumental public spaces, sets off and tempers the dramatic effect of the daring new sculptural forms.

Polshek's feeling for tradition is profound, but never engulfing; his commitment to Modernism is equally sincere, but seldom a resolute insistence. In fact, both sympathies are constantly abstracted and reexamined—at both the personal level of architectural design and the contentious public level of social response. The results reveal a compelling philosophy and a useful method. Whichever principles an architect adheres to must constantly engage the myriad and always challenging constraints the world poses, with the architect tacking happily between noble principles and particular circumstances in order to proceed.

5

6

7

8

13

14

15

16

21

22

23

24

29

30

31

32

Captions on following page

17

Travel Images

1 Hardy House, Racine, Wisconsin. Frank Lloyd Wright, 1905
2 Boiler plant, Illinois Institute of Technology, Chicago, Illinois. Ludwig Mies van der Rohe (with Sargent and Lundy, and Frank Konnaker), 1950
3 Storer House, Los Angeles, California. Frank Lloyd Wright, 1922
4 2400 Lakeview Apartments, Chicago, Illinois. Ludwig Mies van der Rohe, 1963
5 Palace of Fine Arts, San Francisco, California. Bernard Maybeck, 1915
6 Hallidie Building, San Francisco, California. Willis Polk, 1918
7 Seventeenth-century church, Petäjävesi, Finland
8 Spøtrup Slot, Denmark
9 Housing for nurses, tuberculosis sanitarium, Paimio, Finland. Alvar Aalto, 1962
10 Kiehoek Workers' Village, Rotterdam, Holland. J. J. P. Oud, 1925
11 Town Hall, Hilversum, Holland. Willem Dudok, 1930
12 Swiss Student's Hostel, Cité Universitaire, Paris, France. Le Corbusier, 1932
13 Maison de verre, Paris, France. Pierre Chareau and Bernard Bijovoet, 1931
14 Garage, 51 rue de Ponthieu, Paris Villa, Montereau, France. August Perret, 1905
15 Great Mosque of Cordoba, Spain. Begun 786
16 Cave houses near Malaga, Spain
17 Casa Milá, Barcelona, Spain. Antoni Gaudi, 1910
18 Stonehenge, Salisbury Plain, England. Circa 2000 B.C.
19 Fagus Factory, Alfeld-an-der-Leine, Germany. Walter Gropius, 1913
20 The Royal Crescent, Bath, England. John Wood the Younger, 1767
21 Vernacular housing, island of Procida, Italy
22 Ara Ceoli, Rome, Italy
23 St. Ivo della Sapienza, Rome, Italy. Francesco Borromini, 1643–48
24 Piazza San Marco, Venice, Italy
25 Medieval towers, San Gimignano, Italy
26 San Miniato al Monte, Florence, Italy. Mid eleventh–twelfth centuries
27 Horiuji Temple, Kyoto, Japan
28 Zen garden, Daitokuji, Kyoto, Japan
29 Temple, Bangkok, Thailand
30 Pyramid of Giza, Egypt. Circa 2500 B.C.
31 Town gate, Morocco
32 Vernacular housing, Mykonos, Greece

Student Work

1 Drawing exercise. Yale School of Architecture, Fall 1951
2 Pavilion. Yale School of Architecture, Spring 1952
3 Visitors center. Yale School of Architecture, Spring 1952
4 Archives building. Yale School of Architecture, Spring 1952
5 Farmers market. Yale School of Architecture, Spring 1952
6 Financial repository. Yale School of Architecture, Fall 1953
7 Parking garage. Yale School of Architecture, Spring 1953
8 Communications center. Yale School of Architecture, Spring 1954
9 House. Yale School of Architecture, Fall 1954
10 Psychiatric hospital. Yale School of Architecture, Fall 1954
11 Hotel. Yale School of Architecture, Spring 1955
12 Industrialized housing. Royal Academy of Fine Arts, Copenhagen, Denmark, 1956

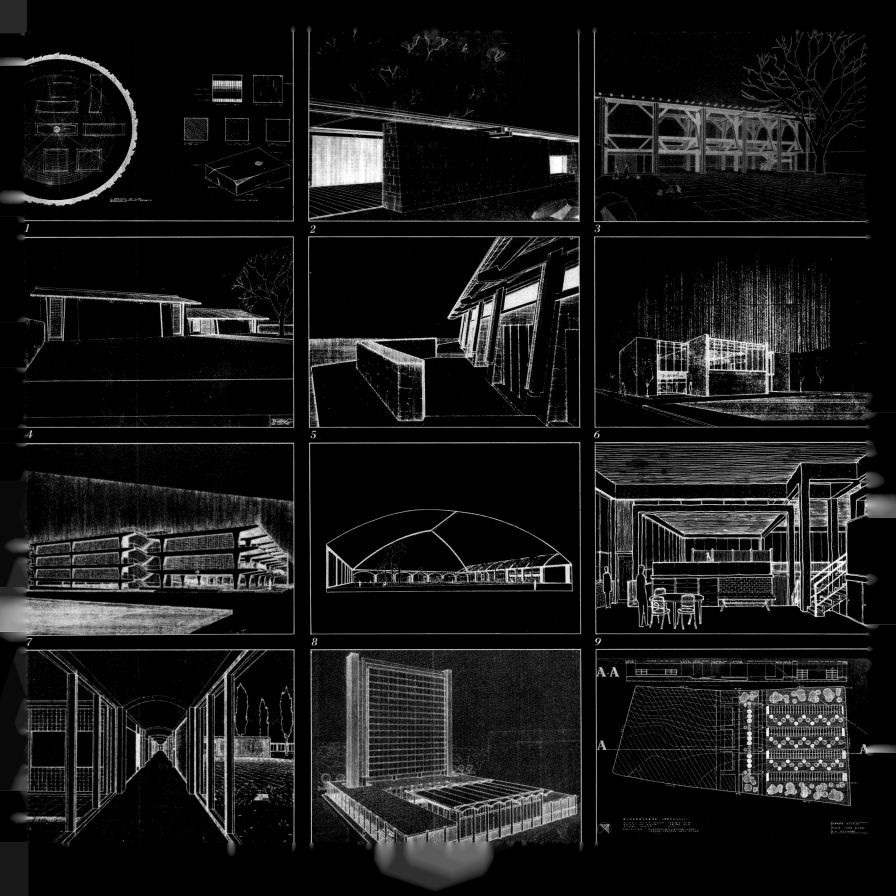

1

2

3

4

5

6

7

8

9

Notes on My Life and Work

James Stewart Polshek

Phase I: Study and Travel

1949–57

The construction in 1949 of a modern house in a nearby upper-middle-class neighborhood of Akron, Ohio led to my interest, and eventually to a career, in architecture. This was no ordinary house. It was designed by the Denver architect Victor Hornbein, who had studied with Frank Lloyd Wright at Taliesin. The flat roof, natural redwood exterior, large expanses of glass looking out on a garden, ribbon windows facing the street, green metal trim, and low profiles contrasted dramatically with the catalog of motley "traditional" styles in the neighborhood. There were stately "Tudors," antebellum "ole manses," miniature "castles," and even one Cotswold "cottage" with a fireproof thatch roof. The Wrightian building mocked its neighbors and made sense to me. I was struck by the rationality of the siting of the house (closed front, open back), the use of natural materials (redwood, stone, copper), and the variation and interconnections of its interior rooms (seven-foot-high spaces juxtaposed with one-and-a-half-story volumes). This house suggested an architecture that embraced the present, an anti-nostalgic dwelling that evolved new concepts of family life and design.

Actually the very notion that architecture involved ideas and meanings— especially that it could be socially relevant—came as a great surprise. This new awareness led to a reexamination of my undergraduate academic objectives. As a nineteen-year-old premedical student, my only "rebellion" had been to major in psychology. An interest in Freud and Jung was fueled by the belief that there were rational bases for man's irrational behavior. This rational/irrational dichotomy eventually became important as a way to mediate between the search for an architecture that was meaningful and one that was based on abstract artistic principles. The only residue of this interest in medicine, and in psychiatry in particular, is the continuing belief that architecture, too, can be a "healing" profession.

The seeds for a career change had been planted much earlier, although middle-class conventions, parental ambitions, and the model of an uncle who was the town's most eminent surgeon pointed to medicine as the career of choice. My parents' *real* interests,

Jessup House

not the socially obvious ones, in fact, supported my new career goals. My mother was a cool, apolitical, highly self-disciplined, conventional yet independent woman. She had studied piano seriously in her youth (but otherwise had no cultural or intellectual aspirations), had worked during the Depression in her own business, and was an absolutist on all questions of taste within the family. As she began to share with me the new vision of Modernism, she cast aside all conventions insofar as they affected the interior design of her home. Out went the overstuffed furniture, in came Mies chairs and tables, linen draperies, Asian artifacts, and indoor trees. Pure white paint and beige carpets appeared everywhere. What seemed to some to be little more than another sea-change in interior decoration appeared to me as tacit support of my desire to study architecture.

My father, by contrast, was emotional, unpredictable, and outrageously radical in his political views—a loner whose argumentative stance often alienated the Akron "bourgeoisie." He was extremely articulate, a self-styled (and self-educated) intellectual who retired at an early age from a family business that he detested. His views were often inconsistent, but on one point he was totally clear: under no circumstances should either of his children go into business. The only life roles acceptable to him were those that were culturally rewarding or socially contributory. Architecture, as a profession, was not understood very well at that time in our midwestern city. But I, and my father as well, soon came to see that architecture definitely was not mere building—that it unequivocally was a cultural pursuit.

House, Western Reserve University

An undergraduate course in the history of modern architecture, taught by Professor Edmund H. Chapman, turned out to be a pivotal experience. At that time, I was a mediocre premedical student at Western Reserve University. Professor Chapman regularly commented upon my ability to comprehend the organizing principles of important works of architecture and spurred my confidence. He introduced me to the pursuit of architecture as a profession and an art form, and encouraged the exploration of a dramatic change in my career plans. Armed with a high grade and laudatory remarks on a final paper in his course in which I "designed" a house to explain the principles of Modernism, I resigned from the pre-med program and was accepted for admission to the School of Architecture at Western Reserve University for my fourth year of college.

The first and only year of architecture school in Cleveland was marked by academic disappointment. Dean Francis Bacon had not yet accepted Modern architecture as pedagogically viable in a university. Instead of Gropius, we studied Vignola. Although I now recognize the importance of an education in classical architecture, it seemed then to contradict all of the reasons for my wishing to pursue this profession. Although I had not yet developed strong political interests, I nevertheless sensed a connection between modern architecture and the public "good" and it seemed that architecture could affect and even change society for the better. If architecture was to be my calling, it had to incorporate new and challenging approaches to design—and to the problems of society. In addition, the school had no national standing and the students were lackluster. In the early spring of 1951 I traveled to New Haven, was interviewed by Professor Carroll Meeks and accepted into the Yale School of Architecture for the following fall.

George Howe

The chairman at that time was the architect George Howe. This elegant aristocrat of the Philadelphia Main Line had "broken ranks" when he joined with William Lescaze and embraced Modernism. His "radical" side generated the brilliant PSFS building in Philadelphia, and the human consequences of Howe's nonconformism attracted him to nonestablishment architects and educators. This led him to support two architectural mavericks at Yale, both of whom greatly influenced my thinking. One was Eugene Nalle and the other was Louis Kahn.

The lesser known of the two, Nalle, was a Texan, ex-building contractor, former Air Force pilot, sensitive painter, and philosophical intellectual. Howe gave Nalle complete control of the first two years of Yale's four-

Eugene Nalle

year curriculum. The last two years of the program were influenced then, as now, by architectural historians who supported an ad hoc visiting critic system of "bella figuras," whose short stints gave a patina of celebrity status to the school but made no pretense of offering an organized education. Nalle's approach was an amalgam of the approaches of three different schools: Taliesin under Wright, the Illinois Institute of Technology under Mies van der Rohe, and the Hochschule für Gestaltung under Max Bill. From Taliesin came both drawing styles (the use of poché, colored pencils, and the Wrightian conventions of representing landscape) and an interest in Oriental philosophy. From I.I.T. Nalle adopted the Jesuit rigor that underlay his constructivist approach to the making of buildings. And from the Hochschule für Gestaltung came the collaborative impetus and the use of paintings as paradigms for architectural compositions.

Detail of Still Life with Pears, *Juan Gris, 1913*

From 1950 through 1953, Nalle, together with his two assistants Lees Brown and Robert Russell, ran the studios as hermetically sealed laboratories. The faculty systematically preworked all exercises and design problems during the summer preceding the academic year. They synthesized the teaching of design, drawing, and technical subject matter in a progressively complicated series of problems, all supported by an eclectic range of readings from Giedion to Spengler and Ortega y Gasset. This sometimes mystical, insular, and intensely intellectual atmosphere supplied all that had been missing in Ohio, and I struggled with much enthusiasm to make up for the inadequate prior education. Everything was prescribed: the sheet sizes (18″ by 21″), the lettering (Bauhaus typography), and the techniques. Nalle's collection of postcards was constantly passed around to introduce the students to the color, graphic, and compositional strategies of Gris, Braque, Morandi, and Ben Nicholson, as well as other modern masters of painting. Visiting critics were prohibited, and even the reading of current architectural journals (of which there were few anyway) was discouraged. The design programs were given names that denied association with standard building types (a library was an "archive building," a grocery store was a "farmers' market," a bank was a "financial repository," and so on). "Determined originality" was the enemy and the design *process* was emphasized over the design *product*. Nalle's interest in and knowledge of traditional Japanese architecture and construction was great and his dependence upon western precedents was secondary. Also his anti-elitist approach posed a significant threat to the art historians (in particular Vincent Scully), whose beliefs paralleled those of then design critic Philip Johnson, who championed the architect-patron system of the Renaissance over the more participatory, "Arts and Crafts" design approach. As Scully and Johnson's influence in the school grew, Nalle's waned and, after Howe died, in 1955, Nalle's ability to continue to be effective was severely impaired. But his influence on some of us did not wane. During the third year a small group continued to look to the concrete forms of Auguste Perret and Tony Garnier's Cité Industrielle rather than to the currently fashionable "forms" of Mies.

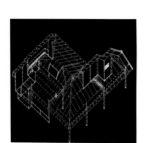

Gepparō Pavilion, detail

Eugene Nalle's influence remains and continues to have an impact on my work. Specifically, my design process involves a series of investigations that include the use of perspective as a central "testing" device. The process also involves moving simultaneously from large-scale planning issues to the investigation of small-scale details, never seeking to perfect any one part of a design problem, but rather moving from one issue to another, refining them with equal care without the sacrifice of the controlling total vision.

After this first year at Yale I married, and while I continued in school my wife Ellyn supported the effort, working there for both the city planner Christopher Tunnard and the painter Josef Albers.

By now a fascination with Modernism included the American master builders. My first trip west of Ohio was the obligatory pilgrimage to the Chicago area during a steaming week in the late summer of 1953. This was my initial viewing of the Modern masterpieces of Sullivan, Wright, and Burnham. Wright's Unity Temple in Chicago and the Hardy House in Racine, Wisconsin, had the

greatest effect on me. The influence of Japanese proportion and detail recalled much that Nalle had spoken of at Yale. The use of daylight in Unity Temple and the dramatic siting of the Hardy House was astounding, though the urbane forms and tectonic inventions of the Johnson Wax complex and the contrasting naturalism of Taliesin at Spring Green were equally powerful early experiences.

In late May of 1954 Ellyn and I drove to California—my first trip west of Chicago. On the way we saw more of Wright's residential work, but it was of a later period and disappointing. More impressive and of much greater lasting influence were the vernacular buildings of the Midwest and the West, the silos and barns and farmhouses, and the mountain resorts of the national parks. San Francisco was our destination, and there after a long search I got a summer job with the firm of Wurster, Bernardi & Emmons. The work was dull, but learning how to ink on Mylar and drink martinis had its rewards. In addition, the beauty and quality of life in the Bay Area, side trips to Big Sur and Ross, and the architecture of Bernard Maybeck and other younger architects such as Joseph Esherick and Warren Callister made the entire visit worthwhile. The trip back through the Northwest, across the northern edge of the country through the magnificent landscapes of Mount Rainier and Glacier National Park, made lifelong impressions.

Louis I. Kahn

If the model of the polytechnic institute was dominant during the first two years at Yale, the Ecole des Beaux-Arts model dominated the last two. In the last year of school (1954–55) Louis Kahn was our visiting critic. Howe had brought Kahn to the school only a few years earlier. Kahn was a builder, whereas Nalle was primarily a teacher, but both shared a highly idiosyncratic and mystical approach to the teaching of architecture. Kahn, of course, was notorious for being on occasion unintelligible—his verbal poetics were often obscure and his scribbled notations usually illegible. But these mysteries stimulated the studio and the work that was generated was as iconoclastic as the man himself. He was at this time attempting to rationalize and integrate a very complex mathematical theory (topology) with his architectural vision. Unfortunately, this resulted in his increasing dependence on abstruse language and frequent absences from the studio. Except for a small group of students to whom he paid special attention, the rest of us were in an almost constant state of anxiety. The early years of a rigorous and systematic pedagogy had given way to an arcane laissez-faire randomness, which was uncomfortable.

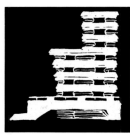

Erich Mendelsohn, sketch

For a senior thesis, I selected a hotel in New Haven without real enthusiasm for the building type. At the final review, Philip Johnson, who was an invited juror, characterized the result as "second-hand" Erich Mendelsohn. What Johnson meant as a negative comment on the work was taken as a compliment. In addition to the Mendelsohn reference, Johnson saw Nalle's influence in the elaborate poché of the drawings and missed the real value of the thesis. In fact, it was the compositional and structural clarity of the scheme, not its graphics or formal expressions, that was important. Notably, almost twelve years later Philip Johnson recommended me for two important commissions. He had always shown an interest in and support for younger architects. During my final two years at Yale he would host private receptions off campus to introduce visiting luminaries. I was present at one such evening when Mies van der Rohe was introduced. These exclusive sessions (those who attended were handpicked by a Johnson protégé) were to be repeated over the years in different formats. In the late 1960s they took the form of gatherings in private homes in which one architect would show a project to the others and an open critique would follow. On one of these evenings I presented an early version of the New York State Bar Center in Albany. John Hejduk, Richard Meier, and Peter Eisenman, among others, were present. The ensuing critique was lively and some of it constructive, but the tone of the gatherings was one of elitism and exclusivity and this was disturbing enough that I declined further invitations. Just after becoming dean of Columbia University's School of Architecture in 1972, Peter Eisenman, the director of the Institute of Architecture and Urban Studies, informed me that he had de-

cided to divide a group of architects into "whites" (the geometric minimalists) and "grays" (the contextualists), and that together they were to be invited to a symposium with the "silvers" in Los Angeles. He asked me to join the whites. I told him that he had misread my work and that I was really not a "white." His response was that I could then be a "gray." My tongue-in-cheek reply was that I was really a "pink" and, further, I did not believe in or want to be identified with any simplistic ideological labeling systems and, in any event, as dean of a school my participation would be inappropriate.

This emerging old-boy network grew and in the late 1970s held meetings at the Century Association, a private club in New York. Later yet, the cast expanded to include a selection of international "superstars," which met in Charlottesville at the University of Virginia (and later in Chicago) for weekend symposia that bore a disquieting resemblance to the secret Masonic Order meetings, even to the extent of using similar code names— P2, P3, and so on. But commercialism finally won out over privacy and both of the proceedings have been published in book form as *The Charlottesville Tapes* and *The Chicago Tapes*. This kind of insularity is ultimately damaging to the idealistic goals of a profession that, by definition, is intended to serve public needs less than private ambitions.

In June 1955, after graduating with honors, the news arrived that I had been awarded a Fulbright Fellowship to Denmark. Because of a Naval Air Corps Reserve obligation, the Fellowship was postponed until January 1956. In the interim my wife and I moved to New York, where I could work in an architectural office while serving weekends. A faculty member had advised me to try to work for Webb & Knapp, a real estate firm that had a brilliant young in-house architect, Ieoh Ming Pei, who was director of design. Henry Cobb and Ulrich Franzen, both Pei associates at the time, hired me as the most junior architect of about twelve people in the design section. Many of the patterns of practice that I observed emerging there I have never forgotten and have adapted to my own practice.

Principal among these was the attitude toward the employees, junior or senior: all were treated humanely and every contribution, no matter how small, was openly appreciated. The pay was not high but our sense of self-esteem was.

In January 1956 Ellyn and I left for Europe on the Dutch ship *Ryndam* to begin the Fulbright year. Despite a journey of eleven rough days we were continually buoyed by the anticipation of this longed-for first trip to Europe. The first glimpse of the continent was the brilliant green coast of southern Ireland under an early morning leaden sky; a day later we landed in Rotterdam. I was amazed by its modern buildings, not realizing that the war, which had ended only eleven years earlier, had destroyed the city almost completely. A train took us to Copenhagen where my project was the study of mass-produced housing at the Royal Academy of Fine Arts under Kai Fisker and his graduate assistants.

The academic year allowed for a great deal of travel. Paris was a magnet, as much for its vivacity as for its architecture. The quiet, toylike order of Denmark contrasted dramatically with the urbanity of Baron Haussmann's avenues. We searched out Le Corbusier's architecture everywhere—from Ronchamp to Nancy to Marseilles and back to the Salvation Army in Paris.

Sénanque Abbey

The great Romanesque monuments such as Vézelay were always more interesting to me than those of the French or Italian Renaissance and the smallest Romanesque chapels in the Dordogne captured my imagination. Later, in the 1980s, a visit to Le Thoronet and Sénanque confirmed these early feelings. This interest in Romanesque architecture was both visual and "political": visual in that the simple arch and vault forms, small-scale cloisters, internal spatial transformations, modularity of the stonework and stylized decoration paralleled my interest in indigenous folk art and architecture; "political" by virtue of the collaborative design and construction processes and the absence of an individual patron and his architect protégé.

Roman Forum

Travels in northern Europe took us to Norway, Sweden, and Finland. In Finland we sought out all of Alvar Aalto's work. In the late 1950s Neoclassicism was not part of the architecture curriculum. Although I saw (mostly by accident) some of Erik (Gunnar) Asplund's work and that of other architects of the early twentieth century, I did not fully appreciate their importance until much later. But experiencing a country in which architecture and design were an integral and meaningful part of daily life was stimulating. I encountered this cultural phenomenon again in Japan six years later.

Toward the end of 1956 we drove to Spain, Morocco, and Italy, where we made many of the marvelous standard stops of a Grand Tour. Fortuitously, we ended up staying in Rome for six weeks. We had longed to visit Greece and the rest of southern Europe. However, our money had run out, our first child was on the way, and the year was at its end. We had to get on with the business of life. On a stormy afternoon in March we sailed out of Le Havre on the *S.S. United States*, vowing to return soon and frequently to Europe, which then seemed (and still does) a most desirable place to live. In New York I learned that Ulrich Franzen had left I. M. Pei and set up his own office and I went there directly. I was hired and stayed from April 1957 until early 1960. It was a true apprenticeship, and Franzen's training at Harvard under Gropius added the Bauhaus to the other educational influences to which I had been exposed. In 1960 our second child arrived and I passed my state examinations. My career was now on its way.

Phase II: Individualism

1957–71

My architectural education, graduate courses in architectural history, European postgraduate work, and the myth of the omniscient architect led me first to approach the practice of architecture in the tradition of the master builder. At Yale the concept of the architect as heroic figure was accepted by most of the faculty and aggressively pursued by architectural historians. Nalle emphasized the philosophies of the great architects, not the formal expressions of their work. Despite our respect for his approach, few of us ever questioned the prevailing wisdom that consistency of style was an imperative. As students we underrated Eero Saarinen because the formal and spatial aspects of each of his projects seemed detached from their immediate predecessors. Yet ultimately, I came to see that Eero was far ahead of his time and that his search for what was special and appropriate for each project did not negate the issue of personal expression but simply relegated it to another level of importance.

During this first period of development as an architect, the master-builder syndrome inspired me to attempt to develop a style by repeating certain architectural devices. For a time I explored the formal properties of building envelopes in such projects as the convex glass exterior walls of the Allied Chemical Materials Research Center; the Quinco Mental Health Center in Columbus, Indiana; and the Old Westbury Campus Service Group. These formal inventions also represented a series of technical and plastic refinements on my part. Issues of appropriateness to context were still considered secondary considerations. Another "signature" of the early work was the tripartite plan and sectional organization of buildings in, for example, the New York State Bar Center, the dormitory complex of the new campus for Choate-Rosemary Hall, and Intermediate School 172. One other characteristic of the work, which actually developed in school and is still present, is a dependence on the Beaux-Arts biaxiality as an organizational strategy. The first and still the most prominent examples are the two Teijin institutes in Japan.

As time went on, an organization was built

that could implement my own ideas and philosophies. I felt less hampered by the need to develop an idiosyncratic and highly personal style. What truly unified the work of this period was the emergence of a conviction that contextual appropriateness and architectonic integrity were more important (and much more interesting) than "style" itself. Of course, common to all buildings were affinities of form, similarities of detail vocabulary, and abstract compositional principles that tried to never lose touch with the humanizing and individualistic aspects of architecture. In fact, I then began to realize that a socially responsible architecture must be indivisible from an aesthetically responsible architecture.

Oster Residence I
194–95

While still working for Ulrich Franzen in 1957 I was commissioned, along with a Yale classmate, Ludovica Schniewind, to design a weekend and summer house on three wooded acres in Stony Point, New York. The owners of this property were ideal first clients. A team of scientists, Gerald and Gisela Oster were interested in the quality of the space as well as the precision of the detail. They were intellectually stimulated by the design process and encouraged our total creative freedom to produce the best piece of work that we were capable of doing. We designed a simple 1200-square-foot rectangular box that enclosed a single space articulated by freestanding elements: kitchen, bath, fireplace, and heater room. The white walls were fenestrated by two different modular openings, each of which had a fixed glass section and an operable plywood vent panel. The ceiling and floor were of wood. Breuer's influence is obvious, but in fact it was the work of Le Corbusier and Aalto, whose buildings I had so recently visited, that most affected me. Le Corbusier's Villa de Mandrot (1930) in Toulon was a particularly important exemplar. The Oster House stood on two parallel concrete linear pilotis, and the floor was reached by fieldstone ramps, stairs, and platforms that grew out of the rocky site and barely touched the "paper-thin" plywood box.

Three years later, in 1960, the Osters commissioned me to design their recently purchased townhouse in Manhattan. The same

Oster Residence II, 74

spatial and organizational strategies were used as in the Stony Point house, but in the interior only. The two curvilinear plaster forms that articulate the ground floor contain a lavatory and a breakfast area. They are arranged on a new tile floor that serves as the dining area and separates the front parlor from the rear living room without interrupting the flow of space. The exterior restoration was my first historic preservation project.

The two Oster houses led directly to major commissions in Japan; two research institutes for Teijin Limited, one of that country's largest textile manufacturers. One spring evening in 1961, I was invited to the recently completed townhouse in order, as Dr. Oster put it, "to meet your next client and go to Japan." He turned out to be correct. I was then thirty-one and working for Catalano & Westermann on the Julliard School at Lincoln Center. Three months after that meeting with Shinzo Ohya, president of Teijin Limited, I was invited to Tokyo where we negotiated a contract. In May 1962 I moved with my wife and two children to Japan to commence a most extraordinarily productive and creative period in my life.

Teijin Research Institute I
196–99

Teijin Research Institute II
200–3

The next two years were an architectural "Cinderella" story, as *Fortune* magazine later wrote. Before "midnight" arrived, two major buildings had been completed—the Teijin Central Research Institute, in 1963, outside Tokyo and the Teijin Applied Textile Science Center, in 1964, west of Kyoto. Each building required areas that totaled over 300,000 square feet and contained facilities for complex industrial research and pilot manufacturing programs. I worked independently with a small staff of Japanese architects, who were drawn from the Kajima Construction Company for the Tokyo building and from Ohbayashi-Gumi Ltd. for the Kyoto building. I designed every detail for both projects, including furniture, lighting, graphics, and landscaping, and selected the artwork as well. I was able to oversee the construction of both buildings and witnessed, for the first time, the almost paramilitary precision of the Japanese construction process. The architect in Japan is called *sensei*, or professor. The respect accorded me was unlike anything I

have ever experienced since that time. If it is possible to be architecturally "spoiled," I was. To have been afforded the opportunity to have the total design responsibility for two enormous structures at so early an age was both frightening and exhilarating. I wholeheartedly accepted the challenge, buoyed by Mr. Ohya's faith in me.

These projects gained immediate recognition by the architectural press, winning awards in Japan and later in the United States. The Kyoto project was featured in *Fortune*, and the Tokyo building was covered in *Architectural Forum* as one of the significant buildings of 1964. The Kyoto laboratory was the largest building represented in the second "Forty Under Forty" exhibition at the Architectural League in New York in 1966. I had left the United States barely known to the architectural community and returned, less than two years later, as an experienced architect with a taste for building at a scale that was almost unheard of for a thirty-four-year-old architect.

One of the greatest rewards of the time in Japan was the opportunity to study traditional Japanese architecture. The incomparable temples and gardens of Daitokuji in Kyoto and the winter palace and grounds at Katsura had easily as great an impact on me as had the architecture of Kenzo Tange, Kunio Maekawa, and Junzo Sakakura (all of whom had been employed by Le Corbusier). My work is still deeply influenced by the proportions, tectonic clarity, and subtle juxtapositions of materials of both the great temples and modest *tsukiya*-style teahouses. Traveling in western and central Japan, I visited farmhouses, *ryokans* (inns), the Ise shrine, and samurai castles. The importance of the relationship of built form to the land was a revelation to me.

We also went to Hiroshima on this trip, where we visited the Atomic Bomb Museum, and met with several American peace workers who were living there at the time. In Tokyo we had observed passionate anti-war sentiments at a rally at a nearby U.S. Air Base and at the Gensuikyo Peace Conference held there during the summer of 1962. The movie-set quality of the "new" Hiroshima, Tange's monument, the hospital of the Atomic Bomb Casualty Commission, the profile of the dome relic (the shattered structure of which survived the blast), and most poignantly, the many scarred, lame, and desperately poor *hibaksha* (survivors), affected me deeply and permanently.

The trabeated north wall of the Tokyo laboratory, the vertical towers with their concrete *brise-soleils*, and the horizontal expression of the interstitial service floors on both facades were attempts to evolve a Modern architecture out of traditional Japanese forms. So, too, was the biaxial symmetry of the plans of both laboratories. The metaphor for the Kyoto building was the samurai castle, complete with drawbridge, defense towers, and moat. The clear expression of the poured-in-place frame and precast concrete infill panels recalled Katsura and the vertical concrete louvers recalled the shoji screens of *ryokans*. The plan of this building is 500′ by 500′ and it is divided by four courts placed around a truncated obelisk. It must be more than coincidence that ninety-three years after McKim, Mead & White's design and twenty-three years after the Teijin building, Arata Isozaki and I won the Brooklyn Museum competition. The museum's original plan was 500′ by 500′ with four courts and a central rotunda—for which we substituted a truncated obelisk!

The magnitude of the design responsibilities in Japan reinforced the master-builder concept of the architect—an altruistic, but egocentric "Howard Roark" image that had been legitimized by art historians and popular culture. Returning to the United States in late 1963, I set up my own office for the first time. In spite of the extensive publicity the Japanese buildings had received, large new commissions did not await me. Working out of my West 9th Street apartment, I did kitchens and bathrooms for friends and relatives, showrooms, and other miscellaneous interiors.

In 1964 John Hejduk offered me an opportunity to teach first-year students at Cooper Union. My studio mates were Robert Slutsky, William Todd Springer, and Sean West Scul-

ley. The famous "nine square" exercise (the use of an abstract field of nine squares as a matrix for two- and three-dimensional compositional exercises) was the core of the program but, as time went on, the total abstraction disturbed me and, in my second year of teaching (and somewhat to Dean Hejduk's displeasure), I broadened the exercise to include a "four square" and a "one square," and introduced the dimensions of human scale and locational relativity. Although the use of "pure" principles was valuable as an introductory teaching tool, I could not divorce my students from a simultaneous awareness of the world in which these principles would be applied. These dual concerns continue to inform both my design work and my teaching.

Loft's Pond Park Pavilion
146

The first institutional commission came in 1965, the result of a chance meeting with Robert Nichols, the landscape architect. It was a recreation pavilion for Loft's Pond Park in Baldwin, Long Island. The pavilion's two wedges of cobblestones, simple tentlike roof, and pocketed barn doors constituted a replay of my first project at Yale under Nalle, synthesized with the vernacular architecture that I had seen in Japan. The pond and adjacent park are in a neighborhood of 1940s frame houses, mostly white, with tailored front yards and screen porches. By relating the pavilion to the natural landscape I was able to detach it from the conventional houses at the edges of the park.

Polshek Office I

In early 1965 the office was moved out of our apartment into a studio that I shared with Richard Kaplan on the attic floor of the Knox Building at Fifth Avenue and 40th Street. A year later, with architects Walfredo Toscanini and Michael Zimmer, we moved to the forty-eighth-floor tower of a building at 41st Street and Madison Avenue. In this beautiful aerie overlooking Manhattan on four sides, the size and complexity of my projects began to grow.

Working out of these two offices, a number of townhouse remodelings in the Upper West Side of Manhattan in New York City were completed. Three of these were of particular interest: the Richards, Williams, and Dunhill residences were laboratories for spatial exper-

Dunhill Residence

Big Brothers Residence
75–77

iments on the interior and an introduction to the techniques of historic preservation on the exterior. In all three cases, the facades were accurately restored while the interiors were gutted. New stairways became freestanding sculptural elements; new floors were created by converting two high-ceilinged floors into three lower-ceilinged ones (Richards); two-story bay windows were added to garden facades (Williams); and cellars were excavated and extended to create new volumes (Dunhill). Each design was adapted to the individual needs and lifestyles of the three families. I also learned about the politics and economics of designing buildings under strict government controls (FHA). Mainly, I developed a strong interest in the interweaving of architecture of two different centuries, which was to become the underlying *basso continuo* of much of the work in the future.

The first substantial work since Japan was the adaptive reuse of a nineteenth-century police station on 22nd Street, which was recycled in 1966 to become a Residential Treatment Center for Big Brothers, Inc. This therapeutic center had both inpatient and outpatient facilities for the treatment of children with behavioral problems. The building was designed in association with Walfredo Toscanini, another classmate from Yale. The treatment center was featured in a 1968 *Architectural Forum* article and, except for one of the Japanese laboratories, marked the first time one of my projects had been published in the architectural press. It was my first major adaptive reuse project, as well as the first nonprofit institutional client. Both aspects of the project represented my belief in architecture as a social palliative and predicted the future direction that the practice was to take.

In 1966 Joseph L. Fleischer came to work in the office directly after graduation from the City College School of Architecture. Ultimately, he became responsible for managing the office in the areas of construction, administration, finance, and personnel—leaving me freer to direct design and to teach. In 1966 and 1967 I commuted to Yale, where I taught a third-year studio under Charles Moore's deanship. Here I observed, for the first time, the student design review becoming an "en-

tertainment," engendered by the writer Tom Wolfe's participation in Robert Venturi's Las Vegas Studio's final review. The edge between populism and elitism was beginning to be blurred. This did not seem to augur well for a rigorous architectural education, which I felt should separate polemics and popular culture from the teaching of the basic principles of architecture.

In 1967 two important projects, though never built, symbolized the dual interests that had begun to have an increasingly powerful influence on my design attitudes. The Bedford-Stuyvesant Community Center, like the Big Brothers project, gave me an opportunity to work on a project in which my social ideals coincided with the needs of the client. This further reinforced my belief that an architect could be useful to a community, and that the architecture itself could be a healing force. A second project, the United States Pavilion for Expo '70 in Osaka, demonstrated my conviction that architecture can serve as a vehicle for communication and public education, and that these goals can be served well by collaboration with professionals from the other arts and media.

It would be impossible for me to detach the continual, sometimes unbearable, social and political tensions of the late 1960s from the kinds of work with which I felt most comfortable. Ralph Nader's writings triggered the development of the consumer-awareness movement and strengthened my resolve that building must serve socially useful purposes. The rescuing of Egypt's great monument, Abu Simbel, from submersion in a reservoir, and the tragedy of the floods in Florence, though distant, had an impact on my sense of the importance of conserving our own monuments. The statistics on the dead and wounded in Vietnam served as a daily reminder of the brutal effects of the war abroad and alerted me to the misuse of the country's financial resources on a useless war while our buildings and infrastructure were beginning to decay exponentially. Closer to home, the assassination of Dr. Martin Luther King, Jr., and Robert F. Kennedy, the "bust" at Columbia University and the race riots that tore through Los Angeles, Detroit, and Cleveland made unavoidable an understanding of the disastrous effects of racism.

Appropriately, the first project of 1967 was the Bedford-Stuyvesant Community Center. This site was in the heart of a severely underprivileged black community in Brooklyn. The program represented the embodiment of the convictions of Franklin Thomas, President of the Bedford-Stuyvesant Restoration Corporation, and was intended to provide a mix of cultural and recreational activities where none existed before. This project fit in perfectly with my personal political and social values and came at a time when questions of equal opportunity for all in America were being urgently examined by elected officials, the press, and the public. The design concept was inspired by the limitations of the two-block site, which was divided by a street. The metaphor of the building as a cultural and recreational "bridge" was the governing idea. The cultural facility on one block and the recreational facility on the other were to act as buttresses supporting a pedestrian galleria-bridge running parallel to and over the street below. The different program elements, circulation paths, and structural/mechanical systems formed highly expressive, integrated building elements that expressed the optimism of the client and the hopes for the rebirth of this depressed neighborhood. Tragically, the assassinations of Dr. Martin Luther King, Jr. and Robert F. Kennedy spelled the end of the project and the end of many dreams. Both the funding and the political support for it disappeared.

A limited competition for the U.S. Pavilion for Expo '70 in 1967 called for a unique collaboration of architects with graphic and exhibition designers, filmmakers, writers, and structural engineers. All disciplines had to unite around one large idea that, in itself, was a synthesis of communications and physical form. The 500-foot-square "egg-crate" structure would be supported over a vast open space displaying conventional United States agricultural and industrial products. This elevated space frame above contained 600 ten-foot-diameter fiberglass spheres, to which small groups of five or six people would retire from the fair and tune into satel-

Bedford-Stuyvesant Center
164

Expo '70 Pavilion
62–63

lite-televised "real-time" unedited events as they happened in the United States, taking advantage of the thirteen-hour time difference. Communication was the essence of the pavilion itself, the unedited events to the world at large revealing the openness of our society—its faults as well as its greatness.

The Donovan Pool House on Sands Point, Long Island, of 1967, provided an opportunity to interpret, in Western construction techniques and materials, a traditional Japanese teahouse. Mr. and Mrs. Hedley Donovan had returned from a trip to Japan and wanted a small pavilion by their pool in the spirit of a Japanese teahouse. Walter McQuade, the architectural critic at *Fortune*, recommended me because of my Japanese experience. Considerations of climate (not enough humidity) and the impossibility of obtaining carpenters skilled in Japanese techniques led me to attempt a non-literal impressionistic *tsukiya*-style teahouse. The aspects of the design that were directly inspired by Japanese architecture were the triple square interlocking plan, the literal separation and expression of support elements, span members, and building envelope, and the emphasis on connective details. Equally important was the placement of the pavilion, elevated above the ground, in the landscape on an extremely restricted area between a road and the existing pool.

In 1968 Philip Johnson recommended me to Whitney North Seymour, Jr., who was on the building committee of the New York State Bar Association in Albany. The project that resulted was the New York State Bar Center. This organization of 30,000 attorneys required a facility for their expanding library, membership activities, and grievance procedures, one that would be located as close to the judicial and governmental center of Albany as possible. This turned out to be a seminal undertaking, the first in a long line of designs that added twentieth-century architecture directly onto a nineteenth-century architecture, using the new to "reinforce" and "repair" a historic set of buildings. The project was at the center of one of the earliest public historic-preservation controversies in New York state because originally the Asso-

Donovan Pool House
204–5

New York State Bar Center
108–11

ciation had intended to destroy the existing townhouses. Happily, it was possible to use the architectural solution as the healing and mediating vehicle. The front third of three historic townhouses on Lafayette Park, opposite H. H. Richardson's New York State Capitol Building (1876) and his Albany City Hall (1880), was preserved and restored. At the same time, we appended to the rear of these houses an uncompromisingly modern limestone building whose forms related more to the small Dutch-style houses on Columbia Street. In 1972, the year of its completion, the building won a National American Institute of Architects Honor Award, one of the first in which the essence of the design solution was the compatability of old and new.

The year 1968 also brought the first large-scale urban design project, the Atlantic Terminal Urban Renewal Area Plan. This master plan for the vast undeveloped area at the intersection of Flatbush and Atlantic Avenues in Brooklyn involved the placement of a new high school, 2,000 housing units, the Baruch School of Business, a huge U.S. Post Office distribution building, and a new Long Island Railroad terminal which became the asymmetrically located nucleus of the entire composition. Elements of the plan were built, including our own 320-unit New York City Public Housing Project in 1971.

Atlantic Terminal Area, Plan
64

The reuse of older buildings for new purposes was becoming more and more common for reasons of preservation as well as the prohibitive cost and poor quality of new construction. A nineteenth-century jail and police station on West 54th Street in the Clinton ("Hell's Kitchen") area of Manhattan was to become the Clinton Youth and Family Center (1968)—a multi-service facility to be operated by the West Side YMCA. The hallmark of this project was the manipulation of the building's interior volumes, during which we rediscovered and restored a vaulted entry hall and made use of "supergraphics" to provide visual order in the circulation systems and identify activities contained in the various spaces.

Clinton Youth Center
78–79

The challenge of designing the building as machine lies at the other end of the architec-

Old Westbury Service Group
206–8

tural spectrum from the reuse of old buildings and new buildings in urban contexts. The 1968 Campus Service Group of the State University of New York at Old Westbury required an almost literal interpretation of program, the accessible placement of systems-distribution devices, a "universal" structural frame, and interchangeable metal infill panels. The panel system and exterior wall profile constituted the first appearance of ideas that would be seen later in the Allied and Quinco projects. This building is contextless—set in the middle of the woods and out of sight of the main campus—and operationally labor conservative; that is, few employees or users. These isolated "machine" buildings, although they do not necessarily represent the political dimension central to my architectural rationale, offer a dramatic opportunity to explore directly the impact of building tectonics on architectural form.

If the Donovan Pool House afforded the chance to study the connections and proportions of Japanese vernacular architecture, the Bronfman Recreation Pavilion of 1969 in Purchase, New York, represented my interest in making the expressive aspects of architecture subservient to the conservation of a valuable natural landscape. Equally important was its compatibility with existing buildings. The pavilion is largely underground. Its sloping roof with its co-planar skylights follows the contour of the site, the brick end-walls growing out of the bermed earth at the bottom to define a patio that is an outdoor extension of the grand living space inside. The use of traditional materials (lead-coated copper, Virginia brick), forms, and details allow the new structure to fit comfortably with the nearby manor house without resorting to the use of Georgian pastiche. The arrangement of structure, mechanical systems, and circulation generates the building's central spine which, in turn, determines its exterior forms and interior spatial organization.

Bronfman Recreation Pavilion
147–49

With the commission of three major new buildings outside of New York State in 1969, the office began to grow exponentially. To accommodate the thirty people in the office at that time, we rented the floor below our forty-eighth-floor watertank studio (at 295 Madison

Polshek Office II

*Choate-Rosemary Hall School, **153–55***

Allied Research Center ***122–23***

Avenue) and added a mezzanine in the original 20-foot high space. The first of these out-of-state projects was a new campus for the Rosemary Hall School in 1969, which was joining the Choate School in Wallingford, Connecticut. The women's school, Rosemary Hall, was then located in Greenwich, Connecticut. The new site was a virgin piece of rolling land on a hill overlooking the Choate campus and I. M. Pei's new Mellon Art Center. The primary environmental objective was to conserve the natural landscape. This was done by siting the four major academic and administrative buildings on a slope down from the crest of the hill that extends into the dense woods below. A 700-foot-long wooden footbridge runs through a forest and over ravines to connect the academic complex with the residential dormitories. Both the academic and dormitory buildings are organized on a 45-degree geometric matrix that depends upon the contours of the topography. Indoor and outdoor stairs, enclosed courtyards, and usable roof surfaces all set at different elevations create a kind of architectural cascade of interior and exterior public and private spaces.

The other out-of-state commission was in New Jersey. The Allied Chemical Materials Research Center provided the first opportunity to use architecture to screen an existing building that, by itself, was a negative intrusion into a beautifully landscaped setting. The challenge was to use architecture as both foil and connector, and to reclaim the integrity of building and parkland. The Corporation's seldom-used 1950s warehouse was to become the headquarters of a new research and development division. The client's mandate was to analyze whether to tear the warehouse down and design a new building or save the old building by transforming it with additions. The latter appeared not only more economical but promised a more imaginative and functional final product. The design concept called for new wings to be connected to the existing building. These would contain the offices of all the professional and technical personnel. The "zippers" between the old and new sections were skylit corridors that admitted light indirectly into the remodeled laboratories located in the existing building.

Quinco Mental Health Center ***150–52***

This strategy of adding these "outriggers" also allowed the old building to be occupied while the new wings were constructed. The basic planning strategies, the design of the envelope, and the attitude regarding natural settings strongly influenced the next project in Columbus, Indiana.

Our work was beginning to be published in the architectural journals. One direct result of this was that the Cummins Foundation of Columbus, Indiana, submitted the firm's name to the Quinco Foundation, a publicly funded community mental health group that wished to build a center to serve the five southernmost counties of the state. The original site selected for the center had a number of major deficits and was accessible only through the service drive of the general hospital. It was located in the Haw Creek flood plain and would have to be raised on pilotis, making access difficult. And the views from private rooms and public spaces would be of the service yards of the hospital and an adjacent nursing home. On the first site visit all this was clearly apparent. So was the fact that the west side of Haw Creek (i.e., opposite the original site) was bordered by a public park, a golf course, and a pleasant residential area—all aspects of an optimistic and progressive social environment. I also learned that the U.S. Army Corp of Engineers had a plan to remove the bends in the creek bed as a flood control measure and, in order to accomplish this, would have to remove over one hundred giant sycamore trees and effectively destroy the park. If the new building could be designed as a "bridge" over the creek, then almost all of the negative aspects of the given site could be neutralized. The users could enter from the side of the creek identified with an optimistic social milieu, and the staff and servicing could take place more efficiently from the hospital side. The building's first-floor elevation could be set level with the higher park and golf course elevation and entered by the public across a pedestrian bridge without steps. And finally, the foundation budget of the building could be used to widen the creek for several hundred feet up and down stream in a controlled manner, thereby avoiding destruction of the park while satisfying the Corp of Engineers. The concept of a "bridge to mental health" was enthusiastically accepted and the resulting building now has views up and down the creek, over the park and golf course. This building as a metaphor for healing remains one of the office's most literal precedents for an architecture capable of simultaneously solving both social and environmental problems without the sacrifice of the client's program or the artistic integrity of the architecture.

Twin Parks Housing
166–69

The New York State Urban Development Corporation, headed by Edward J. Logue in the late 1960s, was, with the Boston Redevelopment Authority (which Logue had also directed), one of the few non-federal public agencies in the United States sponsoring low-income housing of a high design quality. In 1969, we were fortunate to be selected as one of a small group of architects (including Giovanni Pasanella, Richard Meier, Prentice & Chan, and Skidmore, Owings & Merrill) to design new housing in the Twin Parks East section of the Bronx. Initially, we were given six scattered sites on which to place 500 units of housing. The negative economics of spreading 500 units over so many small pieces of property forced us to reconceive the project as a 34-story point tower (for the elderly) and a low-rise ten-story building with three wings, two containing flats and one containing duplexes (for families). Taken together, these two structures formed the eastern gateway to the Twin Parks community. The cladding of contrasting colors of brick (inspired by the Art Deco buildings of the Grand Concourse) caused a major controversy with Ed Logue, whose vigorously orthodox views on modern architecture did not yet allow for an iconography that consciously related to an area context. The different-colored brick stripes created two-dimensional shades and shadows and reinforced the building's sense of identification with the Bronx and its architectural traditions. This was an early use of surface treatment to achieve contextual appropriateness. The danger inherent in this approach became apparent later as the 1970s saw the growth of an empty, scenographic Post-Modernism.

The range of work could not have been dra-

Georg Jensen Store
127

matized more than by a commission to design a new store for Georg Jensen in an existing building on Madison Avenue. This came while working on low-income housing in the Bronx. The construction had to be completed in less than a year, leaving only a few months for design. The principal challenge was to maintain the old image of this staid and elegant Fifth Avenue shop while simultaneously projecting a new progressive one for the future. The "new" was expressed by giant Helvetica letters with the store name incised in sand-blasted aluminum mounted as a huge "entablature" over the new ground-floor storefront. The "old" image was perpetuated by a 7' by 7' pair of cast-aluminum doors that duplicated the original Georg Jensen motif. These were centered in a horizontally proportioned glass wall divided by steel plate mullions and muntins. The interiors were planned on a tripartite system stepping down in size from front to back, where the elevator core was located. The graphic and display inventions, the aluminum-plate ceiling and grid of light tracks, and the various experiments with mirrors and surface treatments were important. Ultimately, though, the project proved to be frustrating because of the exceedingly poor quality of workmanship caused by the pressure of time.

Metropolitan Museum Exhibit
228–29

The Metropolitan Museum of Art had its Centennial in 1969. One of the principal exhibits was entitled "The Rise of an American Architecture" and was curated by the architectural historian Edgar Kaufmann, Jr. I was the exhibit designer and Arnold Saks the graphic designer. The 40" by 40" light-box modules constituted the basic unit of the design combined to form large vertical or horizontal images, all of which were photographed by Elliott Erwitt. The show traveled to seven other American museums where it was reassembled on a black pipe structural framework that we designed to function under almost any condition. The architecture of exhibitry in terms of its importance as a communication tool became another testing laboratory for our building designs. Modular design and transportability were the major technological lessons learned.

A more complex iteration of the building as a

Kingsborough H.P.E. Building, 124–26

"machine" was the Kingsborough Community College Health and Physical Education Building of 1969. The site was an abandoned Coast Guard station on Jamaica Bay in Brooklyn. Although the building was part of a campus master plan, the only requirements mandated by the planners were the masonry unit color and the location of the site. The building's spinal organization separates, on two levels, the large volume public areas (gymnasia, squash courts, dance studios) from the more secure or private areas (pool, administration, classrooms, locker rooms). The use of exposed structural and environmental systems, color, and industrial detailing distinguishes this structure from its neutral neighbors without offending them. No alien geometries or self-conscious material juxtapositions exist to disturb the tone of the master plan. The volume within the larger volume (the dance/squash spaces) modulates the aircraft hangarlike space of the two large gymnasia. The ocean-liner metaphor that can be observed in the linear edge circulation can be traced back to the Japanese laboratories and forward to the Trancas Medical Center and the Glenfield Middle School that occur in Phase IV.

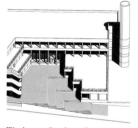

Wesleyan Student Center
165

The Wesleyan University Student Center, a project also begun in 1969 but never completed, sums up this period of growth in several ways: the project incorporated ideas of communication; was constrained by the political and social concerns of the times; exemplified the new contextualism; and used the imagery of the machine for the building's organization. The student center was planned to include such diverse activities as meeting places, dining rooms, a bookstore, radio station, post office, and bank. The prominent corner site was a geographical mediator between "town and gown" during the late 1960s—a very tense political period in Middletown, Connecticut as in similar college towns. The complex was in a highly specific, critical location—facing historic "brownstone row" across High Street. Moreover, this entirely new building was to be built on top of a new underground central power plant for the university. The parti resulted in a taut, essentially opaque facade facing the nineteenth-century brownstone buildings across High

Street. A three-story exposed concrete-and-glass colonnade made up the facade that opened up to a residential neighborhood on the other side. The building was able to serve its many different functions because of a direct plan and sectional organization that allowed for the creation of a primary interior "street." The design was approved and construction documents were almost complete when, in 1972, the stock market dropped precipitously, the oil-embargo crisis occurred virtually overnight, and the project became the first of the recession's many casualties.

In early 1971, just before the recession set in, the first act of the firm's coming transition phase took place. Joseph Fleischer, W. Todd Springer, and Dimitri Linard were named associates. Later in that year Howard Kaplan and Sean Sculley joined them. The pattern for the future was set with Springer and Sculley as associate designers and Fleischer, Linard, and Kaplan as the associate management team. In 1971 I was elected first vice-president and then president-elect of the New York chapter of the American Institute of Architects. I was to become president of the A.I.A. chapter the coming year, but the acceptance of the deanship of the Columbia School of Architecture prevented that. One irony of this transitional period was that I sent a letter to a developer currently constructing an office building on Times Square, who had commissioned an artist to paint his building's soon-to-be-covered steel frame in primary colors à la Mondrian. The letter suggested that spending the money on fees for a more distinguished architecture rather than on temporary decoration would yield better and certainly more lasting results. As a consequence, the developer encouraged his architect to file an ethics charge through the A.I.A. The condition for their dropping the charge was my withdrawal from the assumption of the presidency. However, unbeknownst to them, or anyone, I was on my way to Columbia University—ending "l'affaire Mondrian."

Phase III: Transition

1971–78

The telephone call from Wesleyan University halting work on the new student center ushered in five years that were simultaneously depressing to the growth of the office and stimulating to the development of a philosophy that would unify my political and design ideas. The office shrank from almost forty people in 1971 to eight people in 1974. As the economy severely restricted construction, our energies were focused on keeping the practice alive. There was also time to consider how to reorganize the office when the recession ended.

Quite unexpectedly, my career took a new turn. In 1972 my name was submitted by Max Bond to a search committee seeking a new dean for Columbia University's School of Architecture. After an extensive set of interviews and discussions, President William McGill offered me the position. I accepted, and so began a most enlightening and energizing fifteen years of academic involvement which had profound consequences for the office. The first five of these years coincided with the worst of the recession, affording me the extra time to be totally involved in the revitalization of the school. An interest in education, carried over from Cooper Union and Yale, was now focused on Columbia. With the exception of Romaldo Giurgola's brief tenure as chairman, Columbia's School of Architecture had been declining since Joseph Hudnut left for Harvard in 1937. With the assistance of Max Bond, Kenneth Frampton, Aldo Giurgola, Klaus Herdeg, Richard Plunz, and Robert A. M. Stern, I reorganized the school and a new junior faculty was recruited. By 1975 applications to the school had increased fivefold.

As confidence in the Columbia School of Architecture was gaining momentum, its success was mirrored in reverse by the languid economy and the inactive state of the construction industry. The early days of the deanship provided an opportunity to reflect upon the profession in a way that I had never before had the time to do. The interaction with students, faculty, and visiting scholars, as well as other allied disciplines within the school (historic preservation and urban planning), other architecture schools, and the

Avery Hall

university-at-large, brought about an accelerated change in my attitude about architecture, its theory, practice, and, most important, the responsibilities of the architect to society. One of my first acts was to change the name of the School of Architecture to the Graduate School of Architecture and Planning (fourteen years later, Preservation was added). The student turbulence of the late 1960s and early 1970s had subsided, but the participatory politics, which was the positive residue of that time, still came as something of a surprise. Experience in practice and prior schooling had prepared me for the role of major decision maker, but it had not prepared me for the intensely emotional involvement of students in the defining of academic policies. Weekend-long meetings attended by twelve to fourteen students and faculty members were used to help restructure the curriculum. As the war in Vietnam was winding down, the academic battles of Morningside Heights were heating up. The reform of the school required shifts in faculty and a temporary transfer of responsibilities between the chairman and the dean's respective offices—a stressful but necessary action. During this period, work in both education and practice became more closely aligned than they had ever been before. That is, the social interests of students coincided with the kinds of projects that the office was beginning to receive.

Morningside Campus
70–71

The acceptance of the deanship had several conditions attached, which were enthusiastically agreed to by President McGill: that the dean be named special adviser to the President for Planning and Design; that the dean be allowed to continue his involvement in private practice; and, to avoid the appearance of conflict of interest, that the dean would accept no commissions from the university for at least ten years. The faculty of the School of Architecture had long been ignored with regard to their being retained either as architects of university projects or as advisers on the caliber of buildings to be built and the architects to be selected. The quality of most modern architecture built after the Second World War was appalling, and the urban design of the classically inspired monumental McKim campus was being destroyed. In my advisory role I worked with the campus architect and several members of the faculty as ad hoc advisers. Lists of architects were assembled for each project and the locational parameters for the new buildings were predefined—using their placement to repair, or at least control, the damage already done to the campus. The first project attempted was the design of Avery Library and the extension of the School of Architecture by Alexander Kouzmanoff, an underground solution that had been conceived of as part of I. M. Pei's 1970 master plan. Mitchell Giurgola's Fairchild Center for the Life Sciences created a facade that ended the north-south campus axis east of Low Library and covered the banal Seeley W. Mudd Engineering Building. Gwathmey Siegel's East Campus Housing ended the vista to the east, south of Saint Paul's Chapel, and created a new boundary for the campus. Peter Gluck's addition to the Business School solved the problem of the intrusive and inappropriate facade of the existing building and restored to the east-west corridor between Avery and Chandler the dignity and scale that McKim had originally envisioned. Perhaps the most important new design would have been James Stirling's Chandler North Chemistry Building, which would have completed the northwest perimeter corner of the campus. This superb design was aborted for budgetary reasons, and Davis Brody's more modest, but no less appropriate, Havermeyer extension is now under construction. Kallman McKinnell and Wood's master plan for the Law School may not be realized, but its intentions are consistent with those of the other projects, that is, to add to the volumes of the 1960s buildings by wrapping them with new programmatic functions, thereby completing street walls and restabilizing the primary campus axes. Other projects have restored interiors that had been architecturally vandalized in earlier days. These included Robert A. M. Stern's Jerome Greene Hall for the Law School; Mostoller and Wood's Lewisohn Hall renovation (that did not interfere with the earlier excellent renovation by fellow faculty member Jan Pokorny); Prentice, Chan & Olhausen's East Asian Library in Kent Hall; Cain Farrell Bell's Rare Book Library on top of Butler Hall; Susana Torre's design for the Art History Department for Schermerhorn Hall; Charles Boxenbaum's

Atlantic Terminal Housing
209

Old Westbury P. E. Building
212–13

Bus Shelter

insertion of the career placement office into the base of the East Campus Building; and, finally, my firm's master plan of 1985 for the exterior expansion and interior renovation of Ferris Booth Hall and the first-stage creation of the "Plex," a student center in the cellar of the building.

Thirteen projects were developed in the office during this period, only six of which were actually completed. At the time, the government was the only significant client and our two largest built works were for public agencies. In 1971 the 320-unit Atlantic Terminal Public Housing project at Fort Greene for the New York City Public Housing Authority grew out of our earlier urban design plan. Like the Twin Parks East project, its split tower open-ended corridor plan depended upon the "painterly" use of different colored bricks for its iconography and, like Twin Parks, it broke with the "new Brutalist" tradition of postwar English public housing.

The second substantial project, in 1974, was the new Physical Education Building for the State University of New York at Old Westbury, a former client. The site plan was defined by the campus master plan, which had determined the location and the exterior cladding materials. The program interpretation was constrained by the necessity of observing the New York State Building Code, which is far more restrictive with respect to the relationships of circulation spaces to activity spaces than the New York City code used by the City University of New York. The result was a white, windowless, metal-paneled double box with a central spine that allows for none of the visual integration of observer and participant that so enlivens the Kingsborough Community College project.

In 1971 a small industrial design commission, a prototype Bus Shelter for the New York City Department of Transportation, began as an informal intra-office competition and resulted in a serious cooperative effort. Although only several hundred bus shelters were built, this casual "competition" involving the entire office was important to our future development. It became a first step toward broadening the participation in design by others. My new attitude toward internal design collaboration represented the embodiment of a developing philosophy about the practice. This commission also reinforced my belief that the architect has a responsibility to accept public commissions regardless of the bureaucratic frustrations, low fees, and inadequate budgets.

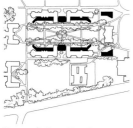

Vassar College Residences

Like many formerly single-sex colleges, Vassar College admitted men in 1969, thereby affecting the distribution and quantity of student residences. In 1971 the administration asked us to study a variety of sites and make recommendations for added new units. As would be the case eighteen years later at Barnard, the primary concern was to use the new student residences to restore some order to a campus plan that had been significantly disrupted by new buildings during the 1950s and 1960s. After reviewing a number of freestanding sites, we learned that Vassar had also planned to restore the interiors of its "Quad" dormitories. Although more radical than just building anew, the idea of using the addition in combination with the restoration seemed to be a solution that could unify the renewed spaces with the added new dorm units and create a more exciting total ensemble. Four new two-story single-loaded corridor dormitories would be literally "clipped" onto the inboard bases of the four drab buildings. The addition would have glass skylight "zippers" (much like the Allied project) over their two-story corridors, which would allow daylight into the refurbished Quad living rooms. No trees would be lost, and the dimensions of the Quad's inner court would be retained. Unfortunately, the high interest rates and oil crisis defeated us again.

Paterson Master Plan
65

Three other commissions further strengthened my convictions about the architect as public servant. The first was the 1971 Paterson Redevelopment Planning Study, for which we were hired by the Paterson Redevelopment Authority to assist in re-evaluating the earlier Gruen Plan, completed in the mid 1960s. The Authority accepted recommendations of ways to breach the ring road (a late 1950s idea that was intended to keep the city center automobile free but, in fact, isolated the center) and restore the connections between the medievalized town center and the areas outside the ring. They also asked us to assist a local firm in designing an auto-supply store and, in so doing, to set higher design standards for other future developments. The result of this collaboration was a great success; all credit went to the locals and we faded back to New York.

Intermediate School 172
170

In 1973 another New York City agency, the Board of Education, commissioned the firm to design the 1,800-person Intermediate School 172 in upper Manhattan. The school was on a site that was part of a master plan developed by Shadrach Woods some years earlier and was located between a decayed section of upper Amsterdam Avenue and High Bridge Park, a place too deteriorated and dangerous to enter day or night. The design concept required that we persuade the Board of Education to allow a reconfiguration of the program; that is, to break the school down into three "houses" of six hundred students each and to arrange these houses so they directly abutted and overlooked the park. The Board accepted the design but the near bankruptcy of New York City ended the possibility of building this school. The perseverance developed in working with a particularly intractable public agency for the purpose of creating a more humane school building was excellent preparation for the increasing public regulation to come.

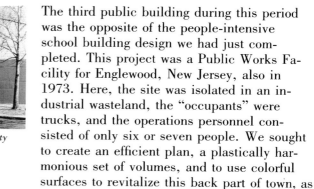

Englewood Works Facility
210–11

The third public building during this period was the opposite of the people-intensive school building design we had just completed. This project was a Public Works Facility for Englewood, New Jersey, also in 1973. Here, the site was isolated in an industrial wasteland, the "occupants" were trucks, and the operations personnel consisted of only six or seven people. We sought to create an efficient plan, a plastically harmonious set of volumes, and to use colorful surfaces to revitalize this back part of town, as well as establish higher quality standards for publicly funded architecture. If we failed, smaller New Jersey towns would be less likely to hire architects of the first rank in the future, so this mundane building type was as great a challenge as any other.

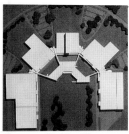

Prototype Turbine Plant
66–67

Later in 1973 we undertook a prototype study for the Westinghouse Electric Corporation in Pittsburgh—collaborating with Westinghouse's industrial engineers in the design of a 500,000-square-foot electric turbine manufacturing facility on a theoretical site. The structural and mechanical systems, materials handling concepts, expansion strategies, and testing of the new OSHA standards distinguished this effort, as did the collaborative aspects of the project. The potential of being teamed with industrial-process engineers had been of interest to me since the time I first read of poets, architects, and farmers joining with aeronautical engineers to design military aircraft for Great Britain during World War II. The idea that the synthetic and intuitive problem-solving process of architectural design could be applied to real engineering problems, not just the "prettifying" of factory lobbies, was exciting. The sixty-page report became the basis for many Westinghouse projects to be built over the next fifteen years. Toward the end of this period two important restoration projects paved the way to our selection for the Carnegie Hall commission five years later.

B.A.M. Playhouse

The Helen Owens Carey Playhouse of 1973 at the Brooklyn Academy of Music provided us with experience in designing and restoring theaters. The Brooklyn Academy of Music playhouse was essentially a straightforward restoration with one major exception: the installation of a new control booth, which technically transformed the theater from the point of view of its practical use without robbing the hall of its traditional character.

Brotherhood Synagogue
80–83

The Brotherhood Synagogue, which had acquired the abandoned Friends Meeting House in Gramercy Park, further honed our preservation skills in 1974. Transforming the 1859 meeting house designed by Kellum and King into a synagogue involved stone "pathology," paint "dermatology," and various "intra-sclerotic" probes (the medical terminology is particularly apt in such preservation projects). A bema, or central altar, was designed at a later date and the only other "modern" addition to the interior was a new light fixture that illuminated the ceiling and walls of the sanctuary. Later, in 1977, we returned to de-

Memorial Garden
80–83

sign a Memorial Garden to the east of the synagogue. The modern garden is juxtaposed with a mid-nineteenth-century building, and we created, by the use of a stepped wall, a forced perspective that narrowed the garden and focused the space on the "altar," or apse at the far end from the street. Initially, the Landmarks Commission found the garden to be "inappropriate" with respect to the existing building. This was my first experience with this commission whose newly expanded staff was just beginning to be more aggressive in asking for a stricter adherence to what they defined as "correct" modifications. In this particular case, "appropriateness" was achieved by doing nothing more than moving the front line of the garden back one foot thus gaining the approval of the Landmarks Commission.

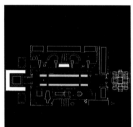

Empire State Plaza

Planning studies abounded during this depression in the construction industry, and two that we completed were important to future projects in the office. The first was a report prepared in 1976 for the State of New York that concentrated on how to make the bizarre, scaleless Empire State Plaza in Albany, New York into a set of lively and habitable spaces that residents and visitors would enjoy. The report was more of a theatrical script than a prescription for physical change. It included recommendations to stock the reflecting pools with fish for Friday night fish-fries; to organize rappelling expeditions down buildings; and to institute "art rides" through the cavernous under-plaza spaces— Governor Nelson Rockefeller's analogue to the underground mall at Rockefeller Center.

Allied Master Plan

The second study in 1976 was for the Allied Corporation, for whom we had earlier completed the Materials Research Center: a master plan for the expansion of its research and development division. In the resulting plan, a series of new wings was arranged to conform to the uphill topography of the site. A new entry lobby and conference center were created at the intersection between the existing, previously remodeled Materials Research Center and the new laboratories. It was a further stage of "repair" of a beautiful, natural landscape that had been nearly destroyed by mediocre architecture.

Simon & Schuster Offices
230–31

The half decade of downward economic drift ended in 1976 when the publisher Richard Snyder selected us to design new corporate offices for Simon & Schuster in Rockefeller Center. Here a client with vision and ambition encouraged us to interpret the spirit of this fifty-year-old publishing company. In searching for formal planning strategies that would define circulation and department location, we used, for the first time, the planning ideas of a late nineteenth-century small "town" to express the program of a twentieth-century corporation. Accordingly, we created a "Main Street" (separating the core from the offices), "side streets" (dividing outside offices from secretarial pools), "alleys" (dead end halls leading to department entries), a "town hall" (executive suite), and "museum" (rare-book room), all of which were built around a formal "town plaza" (reception and elevator core). The Simon & Schuster offices also provided the chance to explore visual perception through the combined use of artificial illumination, large-scale graphics, mirrors, and color to accentuate the appreciation of different spatial sequences. This project was an appropriate bridge between two phases in the development of the office in that it was almost the last project in which I controlled every aspect of the design. This extended, as in the Japanese projects, to the selection of graphics and art works. These interiors remain a continuous source of formal inspiration for current buildings, restorations, and even urban designs.

As more commissions materialized, the office began to expand again and to take on a number of talented younger designers and managers. The generational gap and consequent differences in education and outlook created a second "force" in the office that conflicted, in a constructive way, with the so-called master builder syndrome. My largely intuitive approach to design and my younger associates' greater dependence upon historical paradigms were to have an impact on the work of the office during the next phase, which I call "Transformation."

Phase IV: Transformation

1979–87

As the office began to grow in size again, it became apparent that the different categories of projects—historic preservation, new construction, interior design, and urban design—had to be institutionalized and that we had to develop the expertise that would allow for specialization in these areas.

The political lessons of the 1960s and 1970s—the liberation movements, the educational reforms, the ban-the-bomb protests, the events surrounding the controversial Vietnam War, the feminist movement, and the new environmentalism—influenced my thinking and cleared the way for a further rejection of the authoritarian model of the architect. The example of the Yale years and the decade of individualism were over. My long-held notion of architecture as a social art had originally clashed with the attempt to be the all-encompassing maestro-designer—a definition that was the direct result of my education, not of the utopian and idealistic experiences and beliefs that had originally brought me to architecture. In my early years as dean at Columbia, I was brought in close contact with students whose idealism further reinforced my own predilections but, at the same time, left me wondering how best to translate these beliefs into practice. In the late 1970s, however, the students had become less concerned with both the visual and the ideological purity of Modernism. The idealistic pursuit of architecture was beginning to fade. The students, like the country at large, were becoming more conservative and career-oriented, concerned about future income, conscious of class standing, and, most alarming, primarily interested in style as opposed to design. This had a contrary effect on me. As style for its own sake and its embodiment in the hero architect began to regain popularity, my attitudes about the social mission of the architect were strengthened. The stage was set for a transformation to a more collaborative practice, and an increased dependence on context as the primary generator of physical form. This was perfectly natural since I had always preferred the architecture of the early Middle Ages to that of the High Renaissance. The anonymity of the Cistercian monks, their collaboration and the synthesis of spirit and form expressed in the building of their abbeys had always had a greater influence on me than did the capitalist, patron/protégé model that produced the great Florentine and Roman palazzi.

During this time I became aware that modern architectural practices dominated by one individual rarely remained vital beyond the lives of their principals. It seemed to me that the process of passing on the practice to the next generation could no longer be taken for granted and therefore must be planned for long in advance. This attitude was further strengthened during my first five years as dean at Columbia where continuity of the institution took precedence over any individual's control.

As a consequence of all of these events and influences, the more traditional office or atelier model of master and apprentices began to give way to a synergistic process between myself and the younger designers and managers in the office. The intensity of my direct relationship to different projects began to vary. In some I would formulate the central idea with an associate; in others I would define the general contextual solution and then assume the role of design critic. In still others, I would become deeply and continuously involved in every detail, from concept through interior design.

These younger designers needed the freedom to develop their own unique abilities and their self-confidence, but not their own "styles." However, I retained one prerogative as senior design principal—the responsibility to define the quality and degree of homogeneity of all the works in the office. Here I do not refer to stylistic homogeneity but rather to that of formal and tectonic principles as applied to the different contextual strategies that generated the many different architectural solutions.

It is important to describe the management structure of the office and how the relationship between project management and project design contributes to the overall design quality of the various projects. The current structure of the firm began to take shape in 1980, when Joseph L. Fleischer and Paul S. Byard

became partners. A number of associates were added over the next seven years, two of whom, Tim Hartung and James Garrison, were to become partners in 1987. My role was principal designer. Joe Fleischer served as managing partner, responsible for office and project management, as well as finance, contracts, and personnel. He also managed a number of major projects directly. Paul Byard's responsibility was to develop new business. While our various roles were clearly defined, overlaps necessarily occurred. The associates also had generic, office-wide responsibilities in addition to their daily responsibilities. It is important that each associate be a complete architect who can and often does represent the firm at every level of the project-development process. Together they compose the heart of the firm.

The entire group (partners, associates, and senior project architects along with our office manager) constitutes a "cabinet" that gathers weekly at an informal breakfast meeting. Topics range from commissions received or lost, to personnel and office management, to philosophical questions about the direction of the practice. These meetings have been important to the social and philosophical cohesion of the office. Although I cannot say that all my beliefs are shared by my partners and associates, there is a remarkable but unspoken consensus that service to larger ideals, both social and artistic, is the bedrock upon which this office is built. The result of this non-competitive spirit, which has occurred gradually over the last decade, has produced a consistent quality of architecture more dependent upon response to context than on individual stylistic expressions.

Many of the design associates are more broadly educated as architects than I was. The changes in architectural education, particularly in the teaching of history and theory, and the greater availability of publications of foreign work and criticism have vastly improved the quality of architecture graduates between the mid 1950s and the mid 1970s. In contrast, I have always been an inventor rather than a reinterpreter of historic paradigms. I prefer being the breaker of rules, the maker of exceptions, and the solver of problems. Historic exemplars are interesting as points of departure but of limited use as texts. The conflict between this more intuitive and political approach to design and my colleagues' dependence upon ancient and contemporary buildings creates a creative tension that has energized the work of the past decade and has kept it inventive and harmoniously eclectic, but still responsibly grounded in precedents. The differing types of clients, limited budgets, government regulations, and the variety of contexts often complicate our joint efforts. But these complexities have also caused us to depend upon our collective ingenuities and to necessarily suppress the expressions of our individual artistic fantasies.

The leadership of Joe Fleischer, Jim Garrison, and Tim Hartung (Paul Byard left the firm in 1987), has been crucial to the operations of the office. The management of a diverse staff and the maintainence of the esprit de corps that has always characterized the office largely fall on my and their shoulders. Projects that are both diverse in type and volatile in nature (e.g., completing feasibility studies in four to six weeks; sudden orders from the client to stop or start work; budget cutbacks during design; changes in project ownership; and new governmental regulations) require a high level of flexibility. The talents of these men in the areas of development, design personnel mediation, budget and schedule control, consultant management and client relations are critical to the firm's success. Ultimately, they, together with the other associates, are the communicators and the stabilizers of the office.

Polshek Office III

The fourth phase, "Transformation," began slowly. After the completion of Simon & Schuster and the interior of a small brokerage house, a number of projects came into the office that never were built. A jeweler went bankrupt and disappeared, a competition for dormitories at Skidmore College was aborted, an alternate plan to save a landmark and build a state office building in Delhi, New York, was frustrated by conservative town leadership, and a feasibility study for the renovation of the Ocean State Theatre in Providence never went beyond the investiga-

Trancas Medical Center
156–57

tion stage. But we were expanding again and in October 1979 we moved the offices to 19 Union Square West.

A collaboration with the architect Peter Gluck just after the move resulted in the 1977 design of the Trancas Medical Center in Napa, California. The complex program involved a Seventh-Day Adventist Medical Group, eleven private practitioners, and a psychiatric medical group. The center was to be sited on Trancas Avenue, a piece of highway running through Napa, adjacent to the large general hospital, across the street from a series of small frame houses, and next to a liquor store and a drive-in fast food restaurant. The basic concept was to raise the building above grade, placing all the parking underneath the building. The building came to be called a "drive-in medical supermarket"—an appellation appropriate for California. The building is organized like two ships who have come alongside one another in mid-ocean, their outboard promenade decks being their most public places. Behind are the semi-private spaces (nurse's stations), the semi-public rooms (examination cubicles), and, finally, the most exclusive cells (the doctor's offices). Between the two "decks" and one level below is the open allée, through which cars are driven and patients dropped off at the two primary vertical cores. The program includes a pharmacy, a day-care center, a health club and physical-therapy complex in addition to testing laboratories and an X-ray suite. The ship analogy also applies to the constructional concept, which was basically that of an aircraft carrier, the deck being a reinforced concrete slab supported on slender columns. Because of seismic considerations the superstructure on top of this slab is of wood and stucco. Since the Napa Planning Commission had envisioned this medical center as a three- or four-story building surrounded by an asphalt parking lot, the approval process was harrowing (the planners had even complained about the pastel tones of the stucco). Unfortunately, the exaggerated design-review process of the Bay Area was soon to find its way east.

The final project of 1977 was a modest but prominent restoration of the north wing of the

Urban Center, 84—85

Villard Houses designed by McKim, Mead & White on Madison Avenue. The restoration involved little more than new paint colors, the insertion of mechanical equipment, and the design of a light fixture that created a controversy. The strict preservationists saw it as a Modernist intervention, a defacement of this formerly great patrician house. The Urban Center was dedicated to the exploration of urban problems and their communication to a larger public. The light fixture took on symbolic overtones—a signal to the public that historic preservation projects must encourage a high level of craftsmanship and incorporate sensitively designed new details that contrast with and thereby comment upon the historic architecture without diluting the memory of the original.

Urban Center Bookstore
84—85

Joan K. Davidson, head of The J. M. Kaplan Fund, conceived of the idea of installing a bookstore specializing in books on architecture and urbanism in the Urban Center. The design of the Urban Center Bookstore was begun in 1979. It had to occupy a single available space facing the courtyard, and retain most of its original decorative trim, its elegant proportions, and its fireplace. This little project was an exercise in fitting a small, modern bookstore into an historic room. The fireplace became the sacred repository for rare books. The storage cabinets and shelving and the freestanding table and sales counters completed the furnishing of the room. The irony was that I participated in the creation of yet another home for the architectural publishing explosion that is inevitably leading to a greater emphasis on architecture as a "consumable," making available "catalogs" of modern styles to be copied, further de-emphasizing architecture as a social art and reinforcing the tendency to replace design with style.

Norlin Corporation Offices
234—35

The year 1978 began with the design of a corporate interior in an office building in White Plains for the Norlin Corporation. Here again, as with Simon & Schuster, the logic of the circulation system, the importance of visual termini, varied types of artificial lighting, and the use of internal transparent and translucent planes constituted the basic vocabulary. These elements also satisfied the

New York Society Library
86—87

U. S. Customs House
96

owners' desire to create an office that could function as an art gallery for their collection of Ecuadorian folk art. This was installed by Ivan Chermayeff and was totally integrated with the interior architecture.

The restoration and expansion of the New York Society Library in 1978—the first United States public library, founded in 1754—provided the chance to reorganize this important collection, to restore and refurbish some of its traditional rooms, to create new children's and adult members' reading rooms, and to expand the stacks and administrative facilities. All work had to be done while the library was in operation. Having to undertake significant expansion while the building was in use was not unlike the situation at the Allied Chemical Materials Research Center of almost ten years earlier, and was to recur with increasing frequency in the future. The logistics of building around people is in itself a humanizing exercise, forcing all involved in the process to recognize the asystematic nature of construction, the intricate relationship between time and money, and the importance of human comfort during the process as well as after it.

In 1978 the firm entered a competition held by the General Services Administration of the federal government for the restoration and adaptive reuse of the United States Customs House located on Bowling Green in downtown Manhattan. We entered this competition in association with the office of Marcel Breuer and Associates (renamed, by that time, MBA). This extraordinary Beaux-Arts monument, designed by Cass Gilbert in 1902, was to serve a number of federal agencies to be distributed on its various floors, and a public institution (to be designated later) was to be located in the core of the building, using the grand rotunda and the spaces below and adjacent to it. We chose for the public area the Museum of the American Indian—this option being open to the competition entrants. Using the poché of the four voids surrounding the rotunda, we eliminated their floors at the rotunda level, and created four skylit 45-foot-high atria surrounding the rotunda itself. The subrotunda space opened onto the floor of these four atria and below this floor we inserted a new public auditorium and a series of connections to the subway system. We won the competition and the project is now under construction.

Con Ed Business Office I
232

Con Ed Business Office II
233

Designs for two local business offices for Consolidated Edison of New York were undertaken in 1978. Each was located in a different neighborhood: the first, on East 87th Street, was on the ground floor of a banal new condominium and the second, on West 181st Street, occupied two floors of a decrepit two-story building, which we completely restored and for which we created a new facade. The two projects were commercial, public interiors that encouraged the exploration of stylistic idiosyncrasies. These projects were approached as if they were theatrical stage sets designed to serve efficiently and to delight audiences that we would never see. At 87th Street we utilized tinted mirrors, false walls layered inside the exterior of the building, decorative neon logotypes, brilliant colors, and bands of ceramic tile. At 181st Street we employed cold cathode lighting, grids painted on sheetrock walls, and an entire panoply of interior inventions to enliven the space. These included the serpentine soffits, blue-and-black tile floors, and three butt-joined glass private offices resembling ticket booths for a theater. Any device that would humanize and make more pleasant the act of paying a utility bill or filing a complaint was considered.

Con Ed Operations
215

Following these projects we designed a new West Side Operations Center for Consolidated Edison on 11th Avenue in Manhattan, which had been begun by the company's own in-house architectural staff. In 1978 Chairman of the Board Charles Luce found the design unacceptable and retained our firm to redesign the building without substantially changing the relationship between its interior spaces or its structure. This is not the first time that a chief executive of a quasi-public New York utility had objected to an in-house design. More than eighty years earlier, John Jacob Astor, then an influential member of the New York City Transit Authority Board, had asked that the original design for a large generating station and train-storage building on the Hudson River at 56th Street be rede-

signed by Stanford White. At the West Side Operations Center project we employed a palette of ground-faced block (an ordinary concrete block with one ground face) for the first time to produce surfaces in a painterly manner, implying the existence of shade and shadow, much as we had done earlier at the Twin Parks and Atlantic Terminal public housing projects. The masonry units were used in contrasting colors and textures to make scale transitions, define corners, and to create a lively composition for what was essentially a warehouse and storage building located on a major avenue.

Harlem Shopping Mall
214

The Harlem Urban Development Corporation selected the firm in a joint venture with Bond Ryder James to design a new shopping mall for Harlem in 1978. The block-long, red metal, panel-clad building, to be located on 125th Street, was intended to represent a powerful three-dimensional statement of commercial renewal on this depressed main thoroughfare. The multilevel, serpentine galleria organizing the remaining spaces in the building was connected visually to an existing subway underneath. Here, not unlike the Englewood building, we used color to emphasize the sheer dramatic power of the structure's presence on the street. The project was never funded and remains a "promise" on a billboard on an empty lot in Harlem—deepening the cynicism of New York's black citizens about the real intentions of their elected officials.

Third World Trade Center
68–69

Another unrealized project in Harlem was also to be located on 125th Street. The Harlem Urban Development Corporation wished to build a Third World Trade Center that would include convention facilities, office space for foreign legations and missions, a hotel, a huge trade mart for the display of products from Third World countries, and a restaurant complex that would specialize in the foods of these countries. The stepped vertical forms of the hotel tower contrasted with the horizontal glass-roofed trade mart. Both were unified by a pedestrian scale arcaded base. Unfortunately, the idea and the design remain only a dream—one that should not be allowed to fade away.

U.S. Consulate: Lyons
171

During the Nixon and Ford administrations, the designs of United States foreign buildings were commonplace at best. These followed an earlier period when the State Department had sponsored distinguished design. In the mid 1970s, the Foreign Buildings Office of the State Department, under the leadership of William Slayton, began again to hire first-rate architects. Our firm was commissioned to design a new American Consulate and Residence for the Consul General in Lyons, France in 1978. The site was on a grand avenue adjacent to a series of mid- to late-nineteenth-century urban villas, with Lyons's major public park located at its rear. The placing of a dwelling and a chancery on one site reminded me of one of the works I most admired—Le Corbusier's Maison Jaoul in Longchamps, outside of Paris. The partis bore a very strong relation to that complex of two residences. The iconography of the chancery's street facades was inspired by the nineteenth-century villas on the avenue and its garden facades by the villa's delicate glass-and-steel solariums that faced on to the park. This was the first project in which it was possible for us to synthesize traditional forms with avant-garde expressions on a new building. The Januslike context of park and street supplied the perfect setting. Although the consulate was never built, it became the model upon which the Glenfield School project of 1979 was based. The glass-and-steel design for the garden walls was also incorporated into the Backer and Spielvogel office project, also of 1979. The method used for design review by the State Department was one other notable aspect of this project. A government-appointed board of senior practitioners sits—much like a school jury—to review the designs of proposed U.S. embassies or consulates. Such distinguished figures as O'Neill Ford, Hugh Stubbins, Donn Emmons, Joseph Esherick, Charles Bassett, and others have served at various times. After fifteen years of practice I found reimmersion in design review to be both traumatic and frustrating. The tense interactions between architects of different educational generations and different design philosophies alerted me again to the importance of not allowing oneself to become generationally isolated—as if architecture were a matter of chronological fashion.

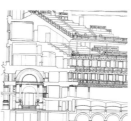

Carnegie Hall Master Plan
88—91

The design was finally approved, but the U.S. Office of Management and Budget terminated it for fiscal reasons.

In 1978 we were selected to become the master-plan architects for the restoration of Carnegie Hall. A shared vision, which included an exceedingly ambitious renovation and expansion, began with a detailed investigation and documentation of this great eclectic building. Designed by the firm of Tuthill and Adler and opened in 1891, the hall had been used not only for concerts but also for commencements and political rallies. This intensive use over almost ninety years had worn the building down considerably and the sound was not nearly as perfect as its reputation led the public to believe. Although a "master plan" sounds very grand, this one was formulated as a series of small packages, unified around three sets of larger ideas. Those ideas concerned the three constituencies of the hall—the musicians, the audience, and the management. For the musicians, the challenge was to expand the backstage facilities significantly, providing amenities that any great concert hall is expected to have, and to restore the stage not only to its original visual grandeur but to its acoustical perfection. For the audience, our charge was to create a graceful and accessible entrance from West 57th Street—in fact, a new lobby—as well as to expand lounge spaces and bathrooms, and to refurbish all public spaces, down to reframing the portraits of performers and artists that line the corridors and galleries outside the performance spaces. A new marquee was also required, the fourth in the history of Carnegie Hall, to shelter and protect, but also to identify and symbolize the hall's entry into the twenty-first century. Finally, for those who manage the complex, the plan provided air conditioning so that the hall can be operated twelve months a year. Our studies also included the pre-schematic design for a new high-rise building to the east of the existing hall, which would provide an additional source of income as well as add a new service wing for the backstage. The architectural expressions of contemporaneity—bronze gridded balconies, marquee, and new light fixtures—were inspired by the existing details of Tuthill's,

Weill Recital Hall Lobby
90–94

Kaplan Space, **95**

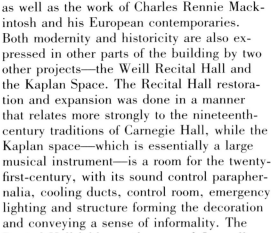

as well as the work of Charles Rennie Mackintosh and his European contemporaries. Both modernity and historicity are also expressed in other parts of the building by two other projects—the Weill Recital Hall and the Kaplan Space. The Recital Hall restoration and expansion was done in a manner that relates more strongly to the nineteenth-century traditions of Carnegie Hall, while the Kaplan space—which is essentially a large musical instrument—is a room for the twenty-first-century, with its sound control paraphernalia, cooling ducts, control room, emergency lighting and structure forming the decoration and conveying a sense of informality. The Recital Hall lobby on the ground floor off 57th Street combines both old and new. The vaults were inspired by the arched, stained-glass windows in the facade and the "new" Carnegie bronze grid was used for the railings and doors in this space. It is here also that we slit the fiberglass-reinforced plaster Corinthian column capitals at the quarter points to reveal an artificial light source inside. This willful move was the visible expression of a distaste, not for classicism, but for the pomposity of its literal application to so vital and popular a place as Carnegie Hall.

Once again we encountered McKim, Mead & White when we undertook the restoration of the Hall of Fame in the Bronx. The original building was designed by Stanford White in 1892. Over the years, the site had become absorbed into the uptown campus of New York University and, later, the Bronx Community College. During that time, this elegant structure fell into disuse and finally was condemned as unsafe for occupancy. The Dormitory Authority of the State of New York commissioned us to develop a plan for the structural stabilization and limited restoration of this landmark. The analytical drawings and conservation techniques developed during our experience with the U.S. Customs House and Carnegie Hall prepared us for this task, which allowed for no new designs.

A newly formed advertising firm, Backer and Spielvogel, retained us to design their new corporate offices in 1979. Not unlike Simon & Schuster, their intention was to establish a new image as a "classical" (not in style but

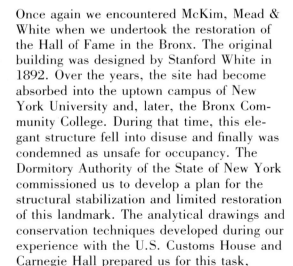

Hall of Fame, **97**

Backer and Spielvogel Offices
236–39

Delafield Estates
160–61

in substance) advertising agency. As in every interior design problem, the most important objective of the program analysis is to find a space or spaces that might be combined to create a symbolic "heart" for the new complex. We selected the area adjacent to the south facade, which faces Bryant Park and views the Empire State Building. Initially, the clients claimed this area for the most important executive offices, but we persuaded the five partners that this space had the potential for becoming the "spiritual" core of their new offices. Using engineering evidence, we demonstrated that south-facing offices would always be hot no matter how much cooled air was delivered. More important, we developed a set of sequential sketches showing that this enclosed public galleria could be approached directly from the new reception areas, that it would afford extraordinary views of the New York Public Library, Bryant Park, and the Empire State Building, and that it could be the province of all employees as well as the ceremonial place to which visitors would first be guided. The interior galleria became the "soul" of the design. On its inboard side we placed all the public spaces of the agency: the library, exercise rooms, wet bar and lounge, boardroom, living room, executive dining facilities, and winter garden. As in the Simon & Schuster project, the corridors were treated as important spaces in their own right, not just as connectors between various functions.

Twenty minutes north of midtown, in the Riverdale section of the Bronx, there has existed for over two hundred years a beautiful ten-acre estate with an eighteenth-century manor house (modified in the 1920s). The English developer, who purchased the site, henceforth to be known as the Delafield Estates, asked us to develop a master site plan, design thirty-two new houses and remodel the manor house and caretaker's cottage and garage. There were two principal challenges. The first was to design a site plan that would restore the formal order of the original man-made landscape, preserve the 256 specimens of trees, and locate the houses in clusters to give them a sense of identity with their immediately adjacent landscape features—all without disturbing the neighbors. The second challenge was to devise a specific formal expression that would feel natural in Riverdale, a community of "stage set" half-timber and stucco Tudor mansions. We studied the architecture of Mackintosh, C.F.A. Voysey, Mackay Hugh Baillie Scott, and other lesser-known late Edwardian architects. Our intention was to derive not a style but a vocabulary of parts from which we could create a series of houses of varying forms in different topographic situations that, while relating strongly to one another, would be able to express an individualism that would certainly be desired by their owners. The project is being completed slowly as the almost surgical placement of the houses requires extreme care with the existing landscape.

Glenfield Middle School
128–31

The Glenfield Middle School in Montclair, New Jersey, begun in 1979, fit perfectly into a typological pattern that had long since emerged in our office: the welding of new buildings to old ones. Once again formal devices and technological expressions were used to mediate between an existing architecture of nostalgia (the existing ersatz Georgian school) and the new architecture of the addition. The latter was intended to express the educationally progressive ideas of the school board that wanted to create a "magnet" school to hasten the integration of the town's educational facilities. In order to add a new gymnasium, planetarium, library, theater, team-teaching classrooms, and community spaces, we first had to remove significant portions of the existing school. The back of the building faced an important public park. However, instead of taking advantage of this soft edge and its views, an existing series of "fingers" projected perpendicularly from the long bar of the school that paralleled the street. In between these projections were unpaved parking lots and service entries. The central idea involved the creation of a new upper level—a piano nobile (as in the Brooklyn Museum eight years later). Under this, all parking and service areas were placed out of sight. Around this new upper deck were located the distinctive forms of the gymnasium, planetarium, library, and theater. The expanded classrooms on the second floor were extruded out as a glass grid behind and adjacent to the existing long bar of the school,

forming a covered entry to the new theater lobby and community spaces from the vehicular drop-off. A blue painted steel structure forms a "zipper" that marks the new entry and continues on to define the theater lobby, then moves into the new library to form a series of skylit reading spaces at its perimeter, and re-emerges on the new deck as a symbolic canopy finally terminating as a portal over the stairs down to the park. The combination of masonry units and ground-face block used in the earlier Con Ed Operations building was used here to even greater advantage, to diminish the scale of the theater's fly and develop a modern vocabulary for the new envelope that would reinforce the traditional one of the existing school.

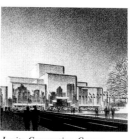

Javits Convention Center

In late 1979, the Urban Development Corporation of New York State decided to build a convention center in New York City. We were asked to undertake a study of what was to become the new Jacob K. Javits Convention Center to be built between 11th and 12th avenues on the Hudson River. Our job was to establish the scope of the project, its urban design guidelines, and, finally, its budget. Joseph Fleischer directed this effort and produced a detailed program and budget that became the basis of legislation passed by the State of New York approving the design and construction of a new convention center. Mayor Koch then requested me to head the panel to choose the architect for the convention center. In early 1980 the panel selected I. M. Pei and Partners. James Ingo Freed, the design partner for the project, essentially stayed with the urban design directions that we had set up, and during the period of design and construction, my partner acted as design and construction ombudsman, assisting in the mediation of conflicts between the construction manager, architect, and the Urban Development Corporation, which was ultimately responsible for the project.

During the planning of 500 Park Tower in 1980, we completed the Securities Groups Corporate Offices within the Pepsi-Cola Building on the corner of 59th Street and Park Avenue. Some of the existing elements of the original Skidmore, Owings & Merrill design were employed, but we also developed

Securities Groups Offices
240–41

a formal vocabulary of gridded interior screens glazed in different ways (opaque mirrors, translucent and transparent glass). This use of membrane-like walls to unify interiors of diverse functions and to screen out less important spaces began with the garden facade walls at the Lyons Consulate project, were then employed at Backer and Spielvogel, and would later be applied in our design for the Amsterdam Rotterdam Bank offices and in 500 Park Tower. The invention and use of this kind of wall had its roots in the Japanese shoji, which allowed for the same type of spatial ambiguity and manipulation of natural and artificial light.

500 Park Tower, **112–15**

This new interior generated our first opportunity to design a high-rise building in the City of New York. 500 Park Tower resulted from the vision of two young businessmen, Charles and Randall Atkins, who eventually sold their interest to Tishman Speyer and the Equitable Life Assurance Society of the United States. The program for the restoration of the existing Pepsi-Cola Building, an icon of modern corporate architecture of the late 1950s, and the design for new offices for Charles Atkins's Securities Groups on the tenth and eleventh floors of that building led to the commission to design a forty-story mixed-used tower. The tower was sited on a seventy-five-foot lot directly to the west of the existing building, between Park and Madison avenues on East 59th Street. The tower was conceived as a singular piece of architecture in its own right but also as a building that would be a backdrop for the elegant integrity of the existing building. The tower also had the urban design function of clearly indicating the east-west boundary between commercial Park Avenue to the south and residential Park Avenue to the north. The parti involved the creation of a granite shaft perforated by deeply set windows. From this stone tower unfolded an aluminum-and-glass envelope whose twenty-four stories of residences cantilevered twenty-five feet over the existing building. The new metal skin was derived from the existing building, but energy laws and technical constraints regarding the sizes of glass and available aluminum alloys required a reinterpretation of the original envelope, the objective being to retain the

proportional subtleties and flush surface characteristics that had always distinguished the Pepsi-Cola Building.

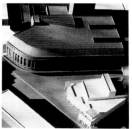

Rochester Planning Study

In 1980, a group of private businessmen, assisted by the city of Rochester, asked the firm to undertake a second-phase planning study of the cultural district in Rochester, New York. The centerpiece of this district is the Eastman School of Music, but otherwise the area is a decayed precinct at the end of Main Street, near the center of downtown. Starting with the original Sasaki plan, we developed concepts for a new theater/cinema/retail complex adjacent to the Eastman School, a 2,000-car parking garage, whose base had to be developed as a lively and occupiable set of retail spaces, and a series of development parcels with design controls that would ultimately result in a unified cultural district plan. A series of pedestrian overpass bridges were designed that would act both as symbolic gateways and all-weather connectors between new and existing buildings. The city required that we work with local architects on the specific designs for a new building for the YMCA and the parking garage, helping them to interpret the design standards that we had created. Unlike the Paterson design experience, there were different levels of cooperation from the local architects. Design regulation, either by bureaucrats or peers, is becoming a fact of late-twentieth-century life, and those who practice in an increasingly populist and educated society must learn to deal constructively with this involvement.

AMRO Bank
242–43

The Amsterdam Rotterdam (AMRO) Bank leased the ground floor, basement, and second and third floors of 500 Park Tower for its New York headquarters. I traveled to Amsterdam to discuss the bank's program with its officers and to look again at Dutch modern architecture of the 1930s to draw upon as source material. In the resulting design the Miesian-inspired free-plan characteristics of the ground floor were retained. During Pepsi Cola's tenancy this had been primarily a public art gallery. The palette of materials and details used on the street floor interpreted, in 1980 terms, the intention of the original Skidmore design. The upper floors of the AMRO Bank, which are more private, depend upon another iteration of the glass-and-aluminum membrane wall, but here the square grid was abandoned for a rectangular one. In every 14-foot module of the two exterior walls a single, custom-designed 24-square-inch indirect light fixture is suspended, so that from the outside the entire glass-and-aluminum cube of the existing building, as well as the lower stories of the attached new building, are unified both day and night without the dependence on the former luminous ceiling.

At the end of 1980 we received a second commission from the State Department, this time to design a new United States Embassy chancery and ambassador's residence in Muscat, Oman. The site, north of the capital of Muscat, was a barren stretch of beachfront facing the Bay of Oman on one side and a dusty mountainous landscape on the other. The assigned area was located in a new compound designated for embassies. Only two or three had been built up to that time. The 70 by 180-meter plot of land called for a building that created its own context. The predicate for the scheme that was finally approved was an Islamic-inspired, complex geometry of open and closed courtyards surrounded by corridors, based upon two interlocking grids. The interior courtyard became a private environmental amenity for staff and administrators of the embassy—the spatial heart of the complex. Another open court separated the ambassador's house from the office building. This courtyard, which acted as a forecourt to the residence, contained a swimming pool for the ambassador's family and the staff. The abstract iconography of the facade, like the formation of the plan, evolved from a loose interpretation of Islamic geometric figures. The elevation consisted of a double exterior skin designed, primarily, for sun control in this extremely hot and humid climate and, secondarily, for security reasons. The outer facade of this scheme was composed of a complicated grid of fiberglass-reinforced concrete screens, infilled with terra-cotta tiles. Shortly after receiving approval to proceed with the working drawings, the State Department stopped the project because of insufficient financial resources.

U. S. Embassy: Oman I
216–19

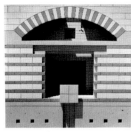

U. S. Embassy: Oman II
216–19

Several years later, in 1985, the terrorist bombing of the Marine residence in Beirut and the volatile nature of politics in the Middle East caused the State Department to reactivate the project. At this time new security and structural guidelines were imposed on all building projects. These rules restricted not only personnel penetration zones, but also the materials with which the building could be built—materials were now considered on the basis of their blast-resistance. In addition, the Sultan of Oman, alarmed at the westernization of the architecture being built in Muscat and the surrounding territory, instructed his planners to develop a series of guidelines for the Islamification of all new architecture. The new security and ethnocentric design standards necessitated a reconsideration of the architecture. The ambassador's residence was removed altogether, parking was eliminated under the building, and the two basic plan grids were adapted to a new set of construction and elevational considerations. The arches and square openings of the new design owe as much to Louis Kahn's aborted U.S. Embassy in Angola as they do to the world of Islam. The alternating colored stone arches, in turn, pay homage to Vézelay and the Mosque of Cordova. The new stone bearing walls, which are blast-resistant, are characterized by stone rustication at their edges. These details bear a direct relationship to the exterior wall openings of the Rochester Convention Center, which was designed shortly thereafter. The Oman project allowed for a degree of plan and sectional invention and a complexity of detailing that would not ordinarily be allowed in a government structure built in a more secure political environment and less isolated geographical location.

Association of the Bar
98–99

The Association of the Bar of the City of New York in 1980 needed to expand its library significantly, and to refurbish and restore both the interior and exterior of its building, located in the middle of the block between West 43rd and West 44th streets and Fifth and Sixth avenues. The exterior of this Beaux-Arts structure, designed by Cyrus L. W. Eidlitz in 1895, although historically important, was not one of great architectural distinction. Our major interest in this commission lay in the opportunity to design new interiors, including new furniture and light fixtures. A new reading room connected by stairs to the existing library, the lobby, and the Whitney North Seymour Room were the principal focus of our work.

Rochester Convention Center
172–75

The final project of 1980 was one of the most important in the office's twenty-five year history. The experience we gained in consulting on the Jacob K. Javits Convention Center in New York City led to our being selected by Richard Kahan, the president of the Urban Development Corporation, to design the new Rochester Riverside Convention Center in upstate New York. The site, located alongside the Genesee River in the very core of downtown Rochester, was a perfect one on which to test the developing design ideas and technical expertise of the office. To the north of the site was Main Street and to the south was an empty lot to be left vacant for future expansion. To the east existed a 2,000-car parking garage, to which we had to add a physical connection, and to the north, across Main Street, a nondescript Holiday Inn, which also needed a bridge connection. The challenge was to place a 250,000-square-foot convention center, the major portion of which is a windowless box, in the center of a downtown area while maintaining the pedestrian scale and without overwhelming the street and existing adjacent buildings. Moreover, the river side of the site faced a restored complex of nineteenth-century mill buildings, which also had to be respected. There existed on the site at the time a bank, eclectic in style but elegant in proportion, designed by the well-known Rochester architect and scenic designer Claude Bragdon. The initial idea was to use this existing building as the principal vestibule and subfoyer for the new public galleria along the river. When we learned that the openings in the granite walls of the bank would not allow for large numbers of people to enter and exit, it became necessary to tear the building down. This raised a modest controversy in Rochester. Since the bank was an isolated fragment, disconnected from any historic context, we received the support of the local preservation society and proceeded with the new design. A new portico, which is the primary entrance to the convention center and its riverside galleria, is intended to evoke the memory of the bank. This light-filled, cavernous glass-and-granite galleria serves as the spiritual and physical heart of the complex. A four-foot-thick granite wall clad in alternating bands of rose and gray granite wraps the entire Main Street and river facades. The horizontal banding of stone and the depth and profiles of the openings in the wall achieve a surface that restores to Main Street a human-scaled pedestrian environment while allowing the building to relate to the nineteenth-century structures and park across the river. The next layer behind the stone is that of glass and aluminum, and, along Main Street, this second "skin" steps down to express the vertical circulation system of escalators carrying people from the garage on the east down to the galleria at the point of entry from Main Street. This stepped facade was a point of great discussion within the design team. My position was that it was more important to diminish the scale of the street facade and inflect toward the entry portico than to maintain the horizontality of the granite wall as it moved around the corner from the river. This was typical of the generational disagreements that often bring my more intuitive visual approach into conflict with the cooler and more rational approaches of my younger associates.

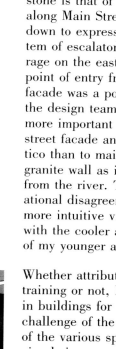

Metropolitan Hospital Suites

Whether attributable to my early premedical training or not, I have always been interested in buildings for the health sciences. The challenge of the complex topological relations of the various spaces and their connecting circulation systems is intellectually compelling. In early 1981, we had the opportunity to design three prototype medical suites for Metropolitan Hospital in New York City. The three suites included an intensive-care unit, an ambulatory-care unit, and a nursing unit. The primary objective turned out to be less one of developing new planning strategies than one in which we explored the use of various materials, assemblies, colors, lighting, and furniture systems to create environments that were optimistic in expression and efficient in operations. The Metropolitan Hospital project was typical of the small commissions that we will continue to do.

During 1982 the office became involved in

Liberty House
176–77

three waterfront projects—one in New York, one in Michigan, and one in New Jersey. The first was Liberty House, a twenty-eight-story luxury apartment house in Battery Park City, the ninety-two-acre landfill area being developed by the State of New York at the southwestern tip of Manhattan Island. The state's rationale for its involvement in the construction of market-rate housing is that the immense profits will be spent on moderate-and low-income housing throughout the State of New York. This particular building is located at the end of Rector Place, facing the Hudson River and outer New York Harbor. The peculiar angle of the west-facing facade was dictated by the urban design plan developed for the Battery Park City Authority. In addition, the authority prepared design guidelines that set aesthetic standards for the base, shaft, and top of the building. In order to reduce the bulk of the structure—made almost unavoidable by the shape of our site—our basic parti prescribed the "de-laminating" of the angled facade, expressing it as a thin layer of light-colored gray brick, hinged at either end by a continuous vertical string of open balconies that connected to the two darker brick corner towers. The design guidelines dictated that the building have a distinct bottom and a top, like the buildings along Central Park West. We complied by creating a gray- and rose-colored granite horizontal base that tied the two dark brick towers and the light brick facade together. The top of the building was intended to evoke the imagery of nautical machinery and the profiles of the uppermost levels of steam ships. The various mechanical contrivances on the roof, such as the water tank, elevator bulkhead, and incinerator stacks are clad in dark green metal and tied together with bands of red and natural aluminum. The Authority did not approve our selection of the light gray brick for the angled layer of the tower. Despite our warnings about the need for contrast, they imposed a brick of a warmer yellow-gray tone and, as we anticipated, the resultant lack of differentiation significantly weakens the overall effect of the building which, nonetheless, sits comfortably on its spectacular waterfront site.

The second waterfront project began with a master plan for a redevelopment of a twenty-

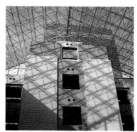

Stroh River Place, **100–3**

one-acre site on the Detroit River, one mile east of Renaissance Center, to be called River Place. The client was Stroh Properties, Inc. The site contains a unique collection of nineteenth- and early twentieth-century industrial buildings and is listed on the National Register of Historic Places. The development combines renovated buildings, restored buildings, and new construction to provide a catalyst for the revitalization of this riverfront district. The assemblage will have commercial, retail, hotel, residential, and cultural uses. The existing streets, service yards, warehouse buildings, and air shafts are being transformed into esplanades, landscaped plazas, mixed-use buildings, and enclosed atria. Vehicular circulation is limited to the perimeter of the site. The primary pedestrian sequence begins at the new River Place clocktower and moves through the entry plaza to the central outdoor esplanade, which culminates in a park at the river's edge that in turn connects with the proposed public Detroit Riverwalk. At the western end of the site, the master plan specifies a location for a future home for the Detroit Symphony. All materials were chosen either to match or complement existing materials in order to create a unified and harmonious ensemble. Brick and limestone are used inside and out, echoing the spirit of the original detailing of the central 1926 Albert Kahn building. While traditional materials such as terrazzo, brick, and granite are used for the paving, custom-made copper light fixtures, the steel clocktower, and metal railings evoke the spirit of the industrial architecture that once occupied the site. The reclaiming of the dignified buildings on the River Place site is a major step in further reversing the trend in urban environments that has been to demolish and build anew. It also demonstrates that a decaying city, like a human wound, can heal from its edges more easily than from its center.

The last of the three waterfront projects is located on the west bank of the Hudson River in Jersey City, within view of our office. It is a 2.5-million-square-foot marine terminal, built in 1929. We were retained in 1983 to convert this mammoth building into back-office space and a retail commercial complex,

Harborside Financial Center
138–39

Peak Competition
220

called Harborside Financial Center. The southernmost of its three sections had already been committed to a banal design of horizontal reinforced precast concrete, and leased to a major New York bank. Our mandate from the client was to redesign the remaining two sections of the building—Plaza I and Plaza II. The solution was to totally reorganize the circulation and to invent a new eastern facade facing Manhattan, whose imagery would reflect the rebirth and conversion of this building. The scheme for the cladding of the terminal evolved from envisioning the facade as a literal "sign" that would be perceived as both a profile and a graphic design from the Manhattan side of the Hudson River. The existing rhythm of the columns and the spacing of the floors created a pattern that emphasized the two complete towers and the incomplete one at the southern end. Alternating bands of aluminum and clear glass are set on a ground of gray solar glass and black mullions and muntins.

The office has not traditionally entered competitions, in spite of my belief that they are intellectually stimulating for the staff and provide the opportunity to work through formal ideas that one infrequently gets to address in "real" problems. The Peak Competition of 1983 was the first major open international competition that the office had ever entered. This was for the private development of a luxury semi-transient hotel and group of private residences in Hong Kong. The site was the pinnacle of a mountain, as the name suggests, and overlooked the harbor and town center. The parti contained three axes—a transverse one that unified the public spaces (lobby, lounge, restaurant), and two slightly skewed longitudinal ones, one of which organized the series of aluminum "houses" that made up the apartments. These grew out of a concrete fortress-like base that contained parking and services. The second long axis organized the private residences, the outdoor recreation areas, and outdoor terraces surrounding the main restaurant. The structures (including the restaurant) were designed as separate pavilions set on a massive stone wall that stepped up and grew out of the precipitous topography of the site.

Resource Recovery Facility
132–35

ADPSR

In 1982 we were commissioned to design the principal public facade and the viewing platform for the North County Resource Recovery Facility in San Marcos, California, north of San Diego. This hundred-million-dollar project will burn garbage from the northern half of San Diego County and turn it into electricity. We invented a small museum to be included in the project, which explains the facility's function to the public. It was our responsibility to make this controversial plant architecturally acceptable to the local citizenry. The project went through three different designs because of changes in program, client, budget, and the approval process. Each scheme depended upon the use of landscape as part of the museum's architectural scheme, which was always contrasted to the industrial forms of the plant. The final design employs earth-tone colored masonry units, wood beams, trellis structures, steel cable, and exposed connections to create the small "trash" museum. After visiting the museum and touring the plant one descends into a lush garden of southern Californian plants and flowers and dense eucalyptus groves, designed to screen the metal envelope of the plant itself. The essence of this project was to employ architecture to explain the employment of high technology to a public concerned about its effect on the environment.

While still working on the North County project I received a letter, mailed to all members of the New York City chapter of the A.I.A., from the architect Sidney Gilbert. It was a "call to arms" that stated succinctly and powerfully that architects have a special responsibility to oppose the escalating nuclear arms race. Within minutes I called him. We had never met, but shortly after our first get-together, we decided to form an organization called Architects for Social Responsibility. We established a Board of Advisers, consisting of distinguished practitioners from all over the country and an executive committee of local architects co-chaired by Sidney and myself. Today the group is called ADPSR (Architects, Designers, Planners for Social Responsibility) and numbers 1,750 members throughout the country. Architects traditionally mediate between the forces of bureaucracy and technology (The North County project being a perfect example), i.e., the politicians and the engineers. The former feign political neutrality and the latter tend to technologically overreach. As history has demonstrated again and again, the fusion of the two can become incendiary. Already we have had a Three Mile Island, a Chernobyl, a Challenger, and countless smaller "impossible" technological/bureaucratic failures. We cannot afford the ultimate failure or there will be no architecture of any kind—past, present or future.

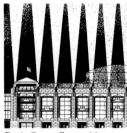

Paris Opera Competition
184

It was impossible to resist entering The Paris Opera Competition of 1983. First, Paris is my favorite city in the world and, second, the building was for music and performance. The triangular site with its point on the Place de la Bastille and the highly specific program constraints regarding backstage amenities, scenery shops, and entry requirements were daunting. We analyzed and accepted the technical program that had been worked out by the competition authors and spent most of our energies on the creation of two facades— the one on the Place de la Bastille and the one on the canal. We saw the challenge as an urbanistic rather than theatrical one, and the difficult exercise was rewarding to all who worked on it, adding to our knowledge of performing arts spaces.

IBM Headquarters
136–37

Late in 1983, IBM asked us to undertake a study to investigate the consequences of increasing the work force of their National Accounts Division Headquarters in White Plains from 1,800 to 2,600. The existing building, of approximately 600,000 square feet, was built in 1968, at a time when IBM had pulled back significantly on its expenditures for building. The structure was covered with asbestos and this was one of IBM's primary reasons for considering redesign and expansion. The existing building was a planning nightmare. Its 1,000-foot-long corridors and lightless offices formed a workplace of unimaginable gloom and dinginess. The new concept again applied town planning metaphors to the design for the reuse of the existing building. The office population was apportioned into "neighborhoods" of approximately forty offices each. Each "neighborhood" was, in turn, served by a "village center," consist-

ing of conference and supply rooms, reproduction areas, and special services. A cluster of "neighborhoods" on one floor constituted a "village," and was served by a single-loaded "Main Street" corridor, either at the perimeter of the building or abutting a new skylit interior galleria. "Side streets" led off the "Main Street" so that all personnel, when leaving their offices, would have a view toward the light—either to the outside, or to the galleria. A "town plaza" and an "entertainment center" were developed, the first being the new public entrance lobby and customer service center; the second being the private employee cafeteria. Between these, on the ground floor, was the "town's" main "shopping mall," along both sides of which, under the galleria skylight, were arranged the support services of the headquarters building, including its sundries shop, post office, bank, and medical suite. Also located along this "mall" were the executive briefing centers— small, self-contained units with conference and dining rooms. A "back alley" service corridor running parallel to the "shopping mall" was connected to loading docks and storage rooms at the rear of the building. In order to humanize the exterior scale of this immense "groundscraper," we devised a scheme that connected three neighborhood modules vertically at their exterior sides by glass-enclosed staircases, around which, at each of the three floors, would be clustered the secretarial pools with access to views and daylight. Above each vertical glass stairway, at roof level, were to be the air-handling units for each three-neighborhood module. This project is characteristic of many that we undertake. It involved the highest level of technical innovation, the re-creation of something new out of something old, and the need to construct major portions of the project while other parts were still in use—thereby dictating an intricate and complex logistical plan for construction.

As 1984 began, we accepted another important landmark preservation and new building project. It was to restore an entire blockfront extending from Peck Slip to Beekman Street on Water Street and is called Seaport West. The client requested us to design a major new infill building in a style that belonged to

Seaport West

Washington Court
178–81

the 1980s but that resonated with the existing adjacent architecture of the eighteenth and nineteenth centuries. The project was initially designed as offices, later redesigned as residences, and was approved by the Landmarks Preservation Commission without difficulty. The exterior elevations of the new building allowed unorthodox juxtapositions of traditional materials that presaged our design of Washington Court.

The site for Washington Court was located on an entire blockfront on Sixth Avenue between Waverly Place and Washington Place in the Greenwich Village Historic District. No major new building had been built there since the area was designated. As in many previous projects, an active and nervous local group created a controversy—before the building had even been shown publicly—that was ultimately resolved with a great deal of patience and the support of a small group of architects, historians, and neighbors. The architect/developer-community confrontation was inevitable. Some residents testified at a community planning board meeting that they needed the existing parking lot. Others wanted a Greek Revival-style building or a Georgian facade, while still others simply did not like the way the building looked. I walked the streets of the Village looking at similarly scaled projects of the past. We examined a number of Greenwich Village buildings whose roof profiles, chimney pots, and decorative detail represented an energetic eclecticism rather than any particular style. The west facade on Sixth Avenue rested directly above two of New York City's primary north/south subway lines and a major sanitary trunk sewer. As a result, the front wall of this twenty-eight-unit building had to be extremely light in weight. Column loading was dictated by the Metropolitan Transit Authority because the point loads of the columns had to be located on top of the subway tubes. Under the zoning provisions of New York City, we could have built a three-and-a-half-story building covering the entire site. In terms of bulk and volume, such a building would have been completely out of character with the elegant brownstones of the two side streets. Therefore, it was decided to observe the following basic rules: the bulk of the building

should come close to matching the height of the adjacent townhouses; the basic material on the outboard side of the building, visible from the three streets, should be a standard brick with limestone, cast-stone, and terracotta trim; and the expression of the apartment volumes inside should become part of the design of the facades. Accordingly, we broke the long facade on Sixth Avenue into three "houses" between the two corners, each of which was defined by a tower before it turned to its short facade on the side streets. If the outer facades were inspired by the Karl Marx Hof in Vienna, the inner facades with their stucco walls and steel balconies owe more to Stuttgart's Weissen-hof. The entire composition, including the twelve-foot spacing of columns, the arrangement of egress stairs on the inboard side of the courtyard, and the configuration of the small but well proportioned apartments, resembled an academic project that had been based on the traditional mews housing type.

Emigrant Savings Bank
140–41

The Emigrant Savings Bank, also located within the Greenwich Village Historic District, one block north of Washington Court, was moving across Sixth Avenue into smaller quarters. Because the bank's architect's initial design had been disapproved by the Landmarks Commission, we were asked to design a new facade. An analysis revealed that the proportions of the existing facade formed a field almost perfectly suited to the application of an Albertian proportional system. The new "abstract" facade derived its traditional bank identity from the inclusion of a flagpole and a clock, conventional features of American banks in the nineteenth century. An interesting irony was that while the community planning board vigorously disapproved the facade design, they applauded the flag and the clock; the bank president, on the other hand, liked the facade because it seemed "progressive," but wanted a digital clock and no flagpole at all.

In 1985, I was asked by the newly formed company of Swid Powell, Inc. to design a series of table objects to be produced for commercial sale. My convictions about the role of the architect as fashion-monger and cult figure were to be sorely tested. Nostalgia for the

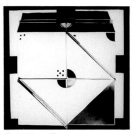

"good design" that the Museum of Modern Art had championed in the 1950s and the opportunity to further refine the interconnection between formal expression and technology at a small scale overcame my initial reluctance to participate. But my early enthusiasm was not sustained as I became increasingly disillusioned by the obvious materialism that these expensive objects implied. I was particularly disappointed when each of us in the stable of architects was given stock white Tiffany dinner plates on which to do a "design," that is, to decorate the plate. At the beginning I developed conceptual ideas for a number of objects: stacked ashtrays, a universal picture frame, a candelabra with interchangeable stainless steel inserts in a crystal base. All of these early designs involved two different materials that were deemed too complicated to produce even for so upscale a market. Sometime later, I completed the prototype for a four-piece sugar and creamer set, which involved the exploration of minimalist forms and Platonic geometries. But, finally, the creation of "name-brand" objects that simply add to the already extensive stock of non-productive luxury items lost its appeal for me. The brief flirtation with "boutique" design quietly came to a close.

Grace Church School
104

The Grace Church School is housed in part of an extremely important ecclesiastical complex designed by James Renwick. In 1985 the school retained the firm to prepare a master plan for its expansion and to rationalize the use of its existing space. This commission added to our roster of clients another old and stable institution that desired to respect its landmark home while incorporating new ideas and appropriate modifications. This study, and one subsequently prepared for the church itself, will be used to guide the future growth of both church and school and will also define the future development possibilities on the church and school property.

A project that has much in common with Washington Court with respect to intense community interest came to life in Bronxville, north of New York City, in 1985. Although Bronxville is not a de facto historic district, it is a village of sophisticated upper-middle-class people who are deeply interested in

Bronxville West
186—87

preserving the character of their town. The project, called Bronxville West, includes approximately 240 housing units, a health club, a 1,000-car garage, and a street level of commercial shops. We began by studying the town plan in general and, specifically, its architecture, both volumetrically and stylistically. The site, located on Parkway Road, covers 3.1 acres, and has at its western edge an escarpment that drops approximately forty feet. Our solution was to design five "blocks" of perimeter housing that are physically attached but appear to be visually separate, each with its own entry from the inner side of the courtyard. The principal challenge during the long approval process has been to find ways (such as graphics, models, comparative history, etc.) to convey to the community that the scale and bulk of the project will be appropriate. Once again, establishing a rapport with the town's leaders and persuading them to trust our commitment to consider their interests will be essential to the ultimate success of this project. Having completed 500 Park Tower and Washington Court, in which the differing interests of developers, architects, and community forces were eventually resolved by the integrity of the architecture, was an immense help to us in approaching Bronxville West.

Coliseum Competition
142—43

As one of seven architectural firms paired with a developer, we created a scheme for re-developing the New York Coliseum at Columbus Circle in 1985. The Coliseum is now empty because of the new convention center, and the tower is underbuilt. By recladding the structures and adding new functional volumes (hotel, health club, apartments, and a retail base), we consolidated the entire ensemble into a seventy-two-story "de Stijl" composition. The relationships of the vertical and horizontal volumes recalled our earlier 500 Park Tower. Our real objectives here were basically urbanistic: to end the axis of Central Park South with a new monumental gateway to the complex; to resolve the centrifugal forces around Columbus Circle caused by the diagonal thrust of Broadway coming from the north; and to stabilize and mark the southwestern corner of Central Park. At the top of the building, we created a "moon" over Central Park—a fifty-foot diameter sphere surrounded by telecommunications aerials and disks—a "decoration mécanique" that would further enhance the splendid profile of Central Park South's skyline as viewed from the north.

Philips International, the developer of Washington Court, returned in 1985 to ask us to design a 168,000-square-foot residential condominium on Eighth Avenue between 15th and 16th streets in the Chelsea area of Manhattan. The site is not in a historic district and the building needed no special permits. We determined that the portion of the complex that faced Eighth Avenue should not exceed six stories, thereby maintaining the basic height of the building wall that flanks the avenue. The tower portion, rising fourteen floors over the base, will be located asymmetrically on and set back from the avenue blockfront. Persuading the developer to accept this particular massing solution was not an easy task. Although the client was uncommonly sensitive to good design, he had, as has become customary today, many consultants—a construction manager, a real estate consultant, a marketing expert, and a zoning attorney, among others. All attempted to convince him that the traditional "wedding-cake" massing would be cheaper to build and that the "bottom line" must govern. We did so precise a comparative analysis of costs that our preferred design prevailed. Although this plan was slightly more expensive, the developer agreed that its appropriateness to the immediate neighborhood and to the urban design of Eighth Avenue as it passed through Chelsea would, in the long run, best serve his interests and those of the city.

The Carnegie Hall experience led us to the Boston Symphony Orchestra and, in 1985, we undertook a feasibility study of the symphony's existing building (McKim, Mead & White, 1891), a master plan encompassing the adjacent annex on Huntington Avenue, and a parking lot to its rear to help them define the physical future of Boston Symphony Hall. The design challenges ranged from designing a counter for the sale of candy and souvenirs to an ambitious scheme that would create a new entrance on the stagehouse side of the building (not unlike the Gewandhaus

Eighth Avenue Housing
182–83

Boston Symphony Master Plan, **117**

Tanglewood Music Shed

in Leipzig). The focus of the plan was to solve the problem of the inverted circulation system that had been created by the Huntington Avenue underpass and that rendered McKim's original formal entry sequence useless, thus causing users to enter the building asymmetrically from its exposed longitudinal side on Massachusetts Avenue. Our solution was to recreate the symmetry and clarity of the circulation, with a new entry that, when built, would become the visual terminus of Massachusetts Avenue as Garnier's Opera in Paris stops the eye at the end of the Rue de l'Opéra. Over the lobby would be a new chamber music hall. Here, as at Carnegie Hall, the troika of interested parties included the musicians and artists, the patrons, and the trustees of the hall, who are ultimately responsible for its maintenance and economic stability. The master plan was accepted by the trustees at a summer meeting at Tanglewood in 1986.

Later, in 1986, we designed a new 1,200-seat Tanglewood Music Shed to replace the one designed by Eero Saarinen in 1941, which was now nearing structural collapse. The changing tastes of audiences and the programmatic requirements of the Boston Symphony's summer season indicated the need for an entirely different kind of building. Saarinen's building was fan-shaped in plan, seating 814 people (using today's standards) and best suited to prelude concerts and conducting classes. The "shed" as prototype seemed to answer most of the symphony management's needs. Its longitudinal plan, expanded volume, 1,200 seats, exposed trusses, extensive use of wood, and the opportunity to integrate balconies on the long sides best suit today's acoustical standards. The new shape will allow the insertion of the larger bulk of the new building into the woods and so maintain a pastoral quality.

The Holocaust had always been an abstraction to me—grotesque, unspeakable, but remote. But this gap was soon to close. In 1985 we were asked to undertake a study for the New York Holocaust Memorial Commission, co-chaired by Robert M. Morgenthau and George Klein, to determine the feasibility of establishing a Museum of the Jewish Heri-

Jewish Heritage Museum
221–23

tage and a Memorial to the Holocaust in the United States Customs House at Bowling Green. However, before we had proceeded beyond the preliminary stage, the Commission decided that the Customs House was symbolically and historically inappropriate for the museum. Soon after, the Battery Park City Authority made available its southernmost site for the museum. The state agreed to lease this valuable piece of property to the museum on the condition that the site also include a thirty-two-story apartment complex. The apartment house would be a nonprofit project built by the Holocaust Memorial Commission or a private developer, with all profits to be returned to a fund for building the museum. In early 1986, before commencing work on the design, my partner Joseph Fleischer and I made separate trips to Dachau, Auschwitz, Yad Vashem, the Ghetto Fighters Museum in Israel, and other memorials and museums from Detroit to Paris. The architectural challenges in this project were formidable. First was the need to create a design that would represent, in a solemn but powerful way, the memory of the 6,000,000 Jews who were killed by the Nazis during the Second World War. A second important objective was to design the museum and memorial so that they would appear uniquely separate and distinct from the residential project despite its physical proximity. The plan calls for visitors to enter from the north, adjacent to the discrete Holocaust Memorial itself. This sixty-foot cube of cast glass and stone panels will be illuminated twenty-four hours a day to symbolize the Eternal Light. A portion of the Memorial's cladding will appear to be partially incomplete. This derives from a semantic relationship. It is an accepted practice to leave a portion of a new dwelling unfinished as a reminder of the destruction of The Second Temple in Jerusalem. The Hebrew word for destruction is *churban*. The same word was an early term for the Holocaust used by survivors. The choice of a monolithic, Platonic six-sided geometric figure is also meant to convey the indivisibility and survivability of the Jews. A seven-story massive stone wall running east and west will separate the public and private realms of the museum. This wall, first perceived from the entry lobby, is intended to recall the walls of

the Second Temple. A cleft in the wall will allow the visitors to enter the prologue. The prologue area will also function as a foyer to the theater that will show a film on the world of European Jewry from the mid-nineteenth century to 1933. The theater will act as the vertical transition to the chronology and core exhibits below grade. This chronology, starting in 1933 and ending in 1945, will be arranged along the wall of a perfect arc (*arc* and *ark* being another semantic and symbolic relationship) illuminated by natural light from above. On the inside of the circle defined by this arc will be a series of smaller specific exhibits dealing with different aspects of the Holocaust. From the end of the chronology one proceeds directly up into the memorial. The interior of the memorial itself is intended, by its quality of light, its immense volume, and its modest but exquisite details, to evoke a mood of profound solemnity, of silence, and of permanence—a physical summary and reminder of how the Jews of Europe once lived, how they died, and how they will be remembered. After exiting the Memorial, one can go up to the section dealing with the aftermath of the Holocaust and up to the second floor for an exhibit on immigration that overlooks New York Harbor, Ellis Island, and the Statue of Liberty. On the remainder of the second floor and on the third floor are temporary exhibits, the library and archival rooms, and the administrative offices. A computer-equipped learning center will be located on the ground floor and mezzanine. Ground was broken on November 10, 1987, the fiftieth anniversary of Kristallnacht.

The musical arts continued to beckon. We undertook a feasibility study for a music shell to be built on a portion of the eight-hundred-acre Bard College campus in Annandale-on-Hudson, New York for the Hudson River Valley Festival of the Arts. Site investigations identified and then analyzed five different locations for the facility with respect to its impact on the campus, parking, walking distances, acoustics, views, and general ambience. The site selected was a twenty-acre meadow overlooking the Hudson River. We developed a freestanding structure whose outboard columns and bow-string trusses, when viewed from the edge of the meadow, give

Hudson Valley Music Shell
224

it the appearance of a large but delicate insect that had alighted on the field. The project awaits the completion of market and environmental impact studies before proceeding.

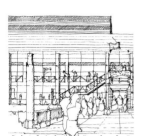

York College Theater
225

The site of the York College Theater, which we were commissioned to build in 1985, is in a section of Jamaica, Queens, New York, that is entering an important period of renewal. The Long Island Railroad is elevated 25 feet above the site at the boundary of a flat parking field opposite a newly completed "megastructural" college-center building. The client is the City University of New York, whose budget for this building is extremely limited. The final parti is necessarily simple: a glass box, three stories tall, will serve as a multiple lobby for the two theaters, forming the principal facade of the complex, and facing the main college building across the street. Behind this transparent volume will be the windowless masonry walls of the theaters. The new theaters are designed to connect to a future outdoor amphitheater. The site plan calls for a circular path of gravel defining the "field" within which the building figure will be situated. This ring will be marked by runway landing lights set at close intervals, which will act as beacons at night and as path boundaries during the day. This kind of project—publicly funded, minimally budgeted, on a barren site, using a building type that is difficult to handle as a formal problem (because of its windowless volumes)—is a common challenge. The odds against creating an "important" work of architecture are great and the bureaucratic review obstacles are formidable. It is presently under construction and is expected to be completed in 1989.

Bard Student Residence
185

Leon Botstein, the President of Bard College, asked us to assist the college in selecting a site for a new student residence in 1985. Construction began in 1987 for a seventy-two-bed complex located in an open field near the center of the campus. An existing dormitory, built in 1959, was awkwardly sited and did not relate to the geometries of the existing roads or paths. Our fundamental site-planning decision was to place the new residential units in relation to the existing dormitory so as to neutralize and absorb it into a larger residential complex, thereby ra-

tionalizing its heretofore isolated and anomalous placement. There was no specific building style on the campus to indicate a formal direction for the appearance of the building. The final design consists of two separate three-story buildings of two "houses" each. The four "houses" have curvilinear parapets and bands of different-colored masonry units, a not-so-veiled reference to the early modern architecture of Vienna. Each has a separate and clearly defined entry. The two-story faculty dwelling completes the composition of new and old dormitories and is cranked off the axis of the new dormitory in order to close the visual gap that appears when the building is viewed from the entry to the site at Blithewood Road.

Barnard Student Residence
188–89

Within a month after starting the Bard project in 1985, we began to design another new student residence, this time for Barnard College. This was to be the first step in the evolution of the college's new master plan, which we developed in concert with President Ellen Futter, her staff, and a student advisory committee. We placed the residence so as to complete a quadrangle at the southern end of the campus with two low-rise wings that fit with the three sides already existing. At the northeast corner of the new quadrangle we designed a nineteen-story tower. Together, the low- and high-rise portions accommodate the four hundred beds required by the program. The primary entry is through a wrought-iron gateway that leads to a covered, but exterior, galleria separating the residence hall lobby from a new café and student service wing. The existing architecture of McKim, Mead & White, at Barnard and across Broadway at Columbia University, and the three existing dormitories called for an exterior imagery that neither rejected the familiar brick and limestone of the existing buildings nor accepted their Beaux-Arts forms. A copper-clad twenty-foot-high rectilinear volume defining the top of the tower contains seminar and meeting rooms that overlook the campus and city. To fulfill the complex program and meet the constraints of the site, including the proximity of Barnard Hall, it was necessary to build a tower without requiring special permits from the city, and, at the same time, to maintain the architectural ambience of this nearly one-hundred-year-old prestigious women's college.

Down Broadway from Barnard is the Union Theological Seminary. In 1985, with the General Atlantic Corporation, we were invited to enter a limited competition for the design of condominium housing to be located on its one-block campus in Morningside Heights. We shared four objectives with our developer clients: that the external visual integrity of the gray stone Gothic seminary buildings along Broadway be maintained; that the internal courtyard/cloister continue to be the sole province of the seminary; that the maximum floor area be concentrated in a location that would have the least impact on the integrity of the seminary; and that the principal entry to the housing would be from the secondary street, Claremont Avenue. The resulting design is a thirty-nine-story tower to which two lower, buttresslike towers have been appended. Our urbanistic objective was to design the tower as an integral part of a neighborhood composition that includes the Union Theological Seminary's twenty-story tower at Broadway and 120th Street, its lower midblock towers, our new Barnard residence hall tower, and the massive belfry of Riverside Church.

Union Theological Seminary
116

The office continued to expand and, in July 1985, we moved from 19 Union Square West to a new 18,000-square-foot office at 320 West 13th Street in the West Village in New York City, about one block from the Hudson River. Here, the associates and partners were able to satisfy both our design preconceptions and our functional needs. The result is more than a workplace. Its simple layout, enriched only with photographs of completed works and drawings of projects, is organized around another "Main Street" that connects the reception area with the partners' offices. A secondary, parallel corridor is open to the studios, separating them from the glass-enclosed associates' offices, which face onto this corridor. The conference rooms, support spaces, print rooms, and master files are located in the central core between the two principal longitudinal corridors. The visual ordering devices of air-conditioning ducts, aluminum-angle frames for openings, and low

Polshek Office III
246–47

studio dividers create a minimalist environment whose crispness belies the relatively relaxed exchange of information and social life that take place among staff, associates, partners, and support personnel.

Metropolitan Park Tower
118–19

The program and site of the Metropolitan Park Tower of 1985, commissioned by George Klein of Park Tower Realty, has so many parallels to the 500 Park Tower project that our being chosen for this exceedingly complex undertaking was clearly no coincidence. The Metropolitan Club, located on the corner of 60th Street and Fifth Avenue, and designed by McKim, Mead & White in 1894, was to be the "site" of a thirty-two-story luxury apartment building. When asked by the developer to undertake this controversial project we requested time to analyze the legitimacy of it in terms of the preservation of the existing building, and to assure ourselves that we could achieve a new building of excellence. We defined four objectives, all of which would have to be met if we were to succeed: 1) to preserve the visual integrity of the Metropolitan Club as a three-dimensional volume; 2) to restore the exterior fabric of the original building and create a fund to maintain the landmark in perpetuity; 3) to create a new building evolved from the proportions and scale of the existing building, using materials and details of a quality appropriate to the landmark—a new building that could stand on its own as representative of the highest attainable standards of craft and design; and 4) to combine both old and new in a harmonious urban design ensemble, completing the stock of high-quality buildings at the southern end of the Upper East Side Historic District. The new tower will occupy the rear yard, and, in order not to affect the interior of the existing Metropolitan Club, it will be supported on three immense columns and by structural walls on the north and east. In addition, we determined that the tower would rise up to the bottom of the crown of the adjacent Pierre Hotel, against which it would be built. It was decided to avoid copying literal details of the Metropolitan Club but rather to rely upon its proportional systems and general detail. The design is a modern building reflecting the formal ideas and available technologies of the late twentieth century. The top five stories of the building and cantilevered flat top owe as much to Frank Lloyd Wright's Unity Temple as they do to Stanford White's club, and the appended bay windows, facing Central Park and south over the annex, are as reminiscent of Sullivan's Monadnock Building as they are of early twentieth-century New York architecture. The limestone-clad building, with its copper trim and implied two-story openings, sits on the existing base of the Metropolitan Club, the new becoming indivisible from the old. The tower incorporates many of the now familiar ingredients that define much of our work: the addition of new to old; the evolution of new formal expressive devices from existing historic ones; the resolution of the technological and structural complexities required by such surgical urban landmark interventions; and the submission to the extensive regulatory and public-review processes that building on the site of a New York City landmark entails.

Sage Hall was built in 1924 on the campus of Smith College in Northampton, Massachusetts and has always been the center of its music education and performance activities. In 1985, the college determined that the building required technical restoration, a reworking of the interior plan relationships, and the acoustical separation of its main auditorium from the practice and teaching floors below. The beautiful cross section of the main auditorium and the relationship of the building to its site demanded that extreme restraint be used in the design and restoration strategies.

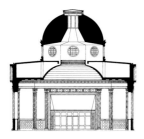

Sage Hall, **105**

Brooklyn Museum Master Plan, **190–91**

In June 1986, our firm, in conjunction with the office of Arata Isozaki, was selected as one of five finalists in a limited competition to design a master plan for the expansion and complete renewal of the Brooklyn Museum on Eastern Parkway in New York City. Isozaki, Jim Garrison, and I met in early July in London, and, working in the basement of the 9H Gallery, developed a parti that became the basis of the final design that ultimately won the competition. This design had as its starting point our conviction that: 1) the original McKim, Mead & White 500-foot-square plan must be expressed in the final master plan concept; 2) that the original center of the plan be clearly identified; 3) that the master

plan delineate a new south facade facing the New York Botanical Gardens; and 4) that the additions not replicate the classical style of the original design, with the exception of one corner pavilion. The preponderant part of the added space program was to be housed in a single new building completing the western facade. The roles that Isozaki and I played were very clear. They represented our philosophical interests regarding the art of building. Isozaki's were in the iconographic, monumental, and representational aspects of the projects. Mine were in the issues of "connections"—both those that were external and urbanistic (the relationship of the new museum to its neighborhood and to the Botanical Gardens), and internal (the relationships of circulation areas to dedicated spaces, both as functional pathways and volumetric transitions). One other "connection" that I focused on was that between the museum plan as originally conceived by McKim, Mead & White and the new master plan configuration that resulted in the cranked plan at the piano nobile level. The museum's original entry from Eastern Parkway will be restored, including the replacement of the original stairs and the addition of new ramps. An eighty-foot-high vaulted gallery space will connect the two entries. From the obelisk two bridges will splay out to connect to the new west wing at third points. The bridges will also form the two sides of the new glass-roofed Rodin Court. The urban design plan extends the angles of these bridges out onto the landscape as open-air promenades, enclosing a major reflecting pool (where, in the nineteenth century, a reservoir had existed) and an amphitheater facing the new west facade. The analytical diagrams used to define the plan and substantiate and rationalize the design were set in London when we first met with Isozaki, and they never changed. During the ten weeks of development after our London meeting we communicated three or four times a week by Telefax and telephone. The thirteen-hour time difference between Japan and New York allowed our teams to work twenty-four hours a day! We are now working with Robert Buck, the director of the museum, and his staff to re-define and implement the master plan without sacrificing the larger vision we conceived.

Yerba Buena Master Plan and Theater

In July 1986, after months of interviews, the San Francisco Redevelopment Authority chose our firm to design a new 800-seat repertory theater in the Yerba Buena Gardens cultural district north of the Moscone Convention Center. Fumihiko Maki was selected at the same time to design a small visual-arts center, and six months later Romaldo Giurgola was appointed as architect for the garden esplanade. Six months afterward, the city of San Francisco decided to consider an expansion of the convention center under the block on which our three projects were to be built. The Redevelopment Agency asked each of the architects to do a brief study reporting on the impact that the construction of the underground convention center would bear on our buildings. Our studies resulted in a severe critique of the original convention center expansion scheme because it had created a second convention center entry at the end of the esplanade and opposite the proposed foyer of our new theater. We (Giurgola and myself—Maki could not participate) believed that we had to suggest an alternative urban design solution. Our new design called for the depression below grade of Howard Street, which presently separates the new cultural center block and the existing convention center block. This single move would permit the two blocks to be unified and would allow a new central entry lobby for the convention center that would be integrated with a monumental fountain to celebrate this new downtown public space and expanded convention center. Our proposal was enthusiastically endorsed by the Redevelopment Authority, and a public bond issue, based on our estimated cost of the new concept, was passed by the voters in November 1986.

At the time of this writing, we are at work on a number of new projects. These include a new mail distribution facility for the U.S. Post Office in Newburgh, New York; an urban design plan and office complex for the center of downtown Schenectady, New York; a 125-acre luxury housing development in Kent, Connecticut; two corporate interiors—one for the Screen Actors Guild and one for the advertising firm of Muir Cornelius Moore; a new housing block and cinema center on Site 11 at Battery Park City; a forty-story apartment tower for the General Atlantic Corporation on the upper east side of Manhattan; the Drawing Center in the Soho section of New York City; the renovation of George Washington Hall at the Phillips Andover Academy in Massachusetts, and the addition of a new theater to the existing building; a new studio theater and support space at Oberlin College; a master plan and new science facility at Brooklyn College; a plan for a "new town" in Arverne, Queens on the Atlantic Ocean; a mission for the German Democratic Republic in New York City; and a Civic Center for Kingsport, Tennessee.

On June 30 1987, after fifteen years, I retired as Dean of the Faculty of Architecture, Planning, and Preservation at Columbia University. I shall remain as Professor of Architecture, teaching design and, of course, will continue to devote myself to the practice of architecture.

The work of our firm evolves not from a search for style but from a response to context. Our commitment to design each project appropriately to fulfill a spectrum of human needs remains fundamental. Stylistic labels such as Post-Modern or Neo-Modern do not apply to the work that we do. Rather, the core of the practice continues to be the quest to create a morally and aesthetically responsible architecture.

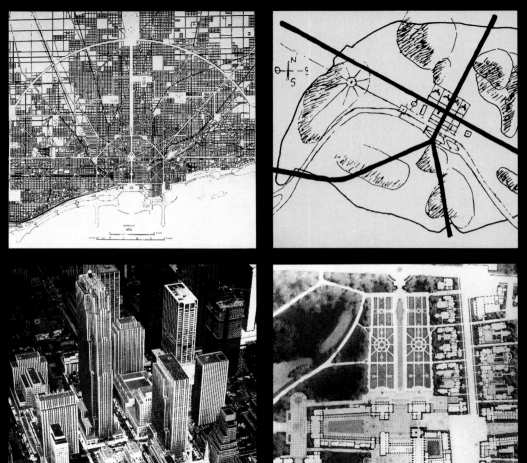

Urban Design

"Urban design" as used here is a convenient, but not entirely accurate, term for projects and studies at scales larger than those of the individual building. Not all of those contained in this section are urban, but all do involve the design of large and more than ordinarily complex systems for human use.

The U.S. Pavilion for Expo '70 (1967) and the Westinghouse Prototype Turbine Plant (1973) were visions of the future—the former in terms of architecture and communication, the latter with respect to the technology of manufacturing processes and their effect on workers. The Paterson, New Jersey Master Plan (1971), the Atlantic Terminal Urban Renewal Area Concept Plan (1968), the Third World Trade Center (1978), the Rochester Cultural District Planning Study (1980), and the Schenectady Downtown Plan (1986) are more conventional urban design projects involving the setting of two- and three-dimensional design guidelines for the future development of a part of a city. The Allied Master Plan (1976) is a private corporate development plan for research and development "zones." And, finally, the work for the Morningside Campus Plan of Columbia University (1972–87) could well have fallen into either the category entitled "Reinforcement" or the one entitled "Reparation" in that the essence of my role was to suggest locations for new projects that would reunify the campus. My position in these university projects was not as designer but as consultant to the president of the university. As adviser over a fifteen-year period (first for President William J. McGill and later for President Michael I. Sovern) I submitted lists of names of qualified architects to design new buildings and renovations. The intention was to try to repair the errors of the 1950s and 1960s and, in so doing, to reinforce the best qualities of McKim, Mead & White's original plan.

In general, I see no difference between urban design and architecture. The governing formal principles are the same and the public service obligation is as important in urban design as it is in the design of any small building that is visually or functionally accessible to the public.

---

1 Plan. Chicago, Illinois. Daniel Burnham and Edward Bennett, 1909
2 Plan. Le Corbusier's grande croisée, Paris, France. 1937
3 Rockefeller Center, New York. Raymond Hood, Wallace Harrison, and others, 1931–39
4 Plan. Cranbrook Academy of Art, Bloomfield Hills, Michigan. Eliel Saarinen, 1925

U.S. Pavilion for Expo '70
invited competition
Osaka, Japan, 1967
Client: United States Information Agency,
Washington, D.C.
with: Arnold Saks (graphic designer)

1 Site plan
2 Approach
3 Escalator up
4 At the pod
5 Top arrival
6 Plan
7 Pod detail. Plan and section
8 Pavilion cross sections

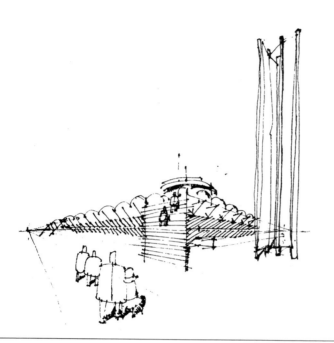

2

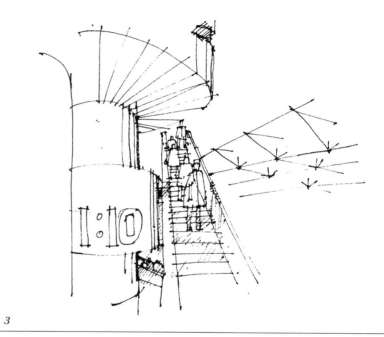

3

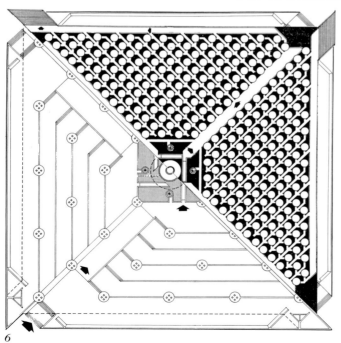

6

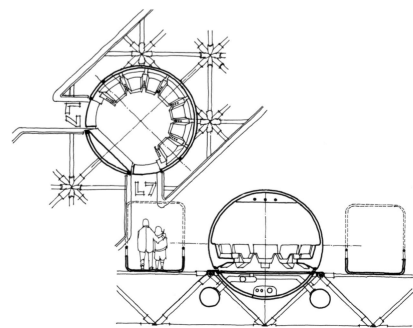

7

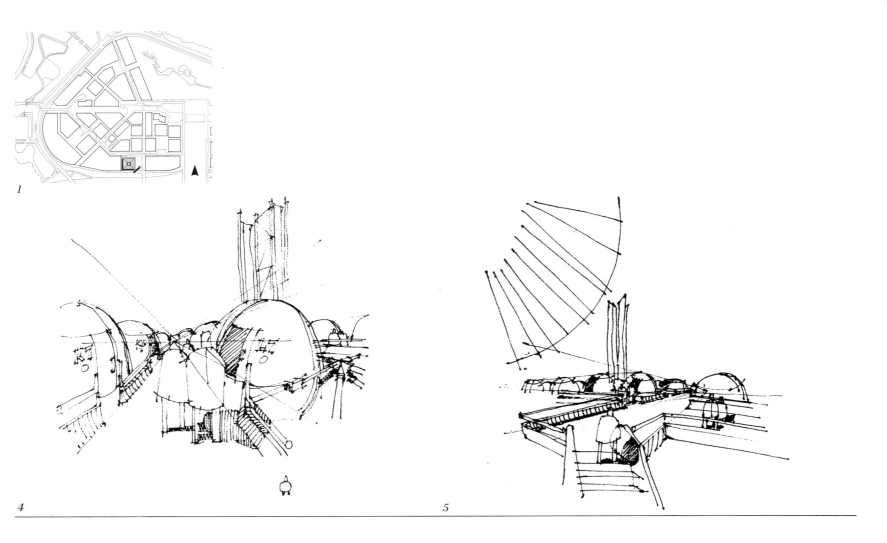

1

4

5

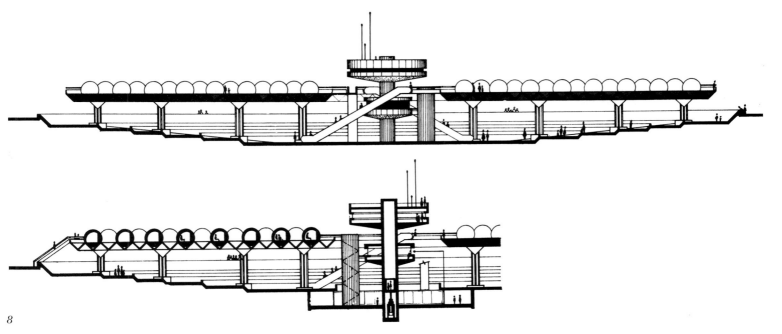

8

63

Atlantic Terminal Urban Renewal Area
Concept Plan   *study*
Brooklyn, New York, 1968
Client: Housing Development Authority,
New York, New York

1 Model of area from west
2 Site plan

1

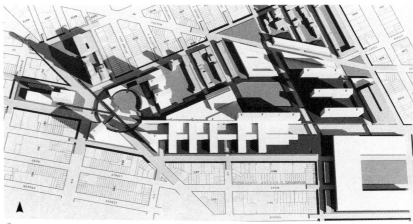

2

Paterson, New Jersey Master Plan *study*
Paterson, New Jersey, 1971
Client: Paterson Redevelopment Authority
with: W. Todd Springer, Sean W. Sculley

1 *Model*
2 *Center city site plan*
3 *Overall view*

1

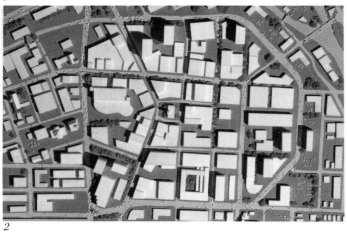

2

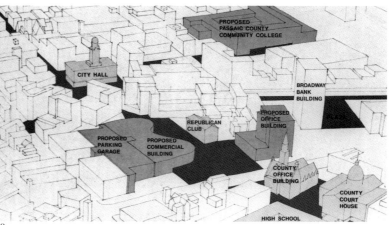

3

Westinghouse Prototype Turbine Plant
study, 1973
Client: Westinghouse Electric Corporation,
Pittsburgh, Pennsylvania
with: Joseph L. Fleischer, Sean W. Sculley

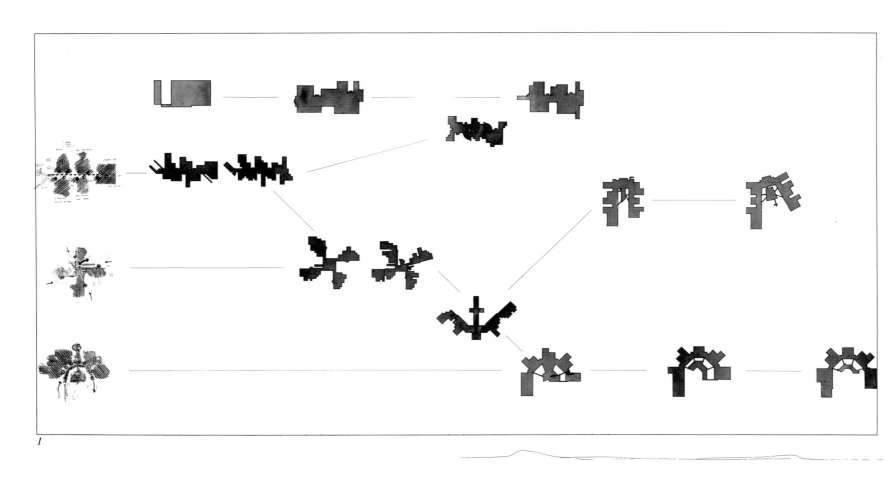

1

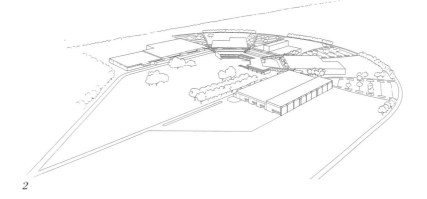

2

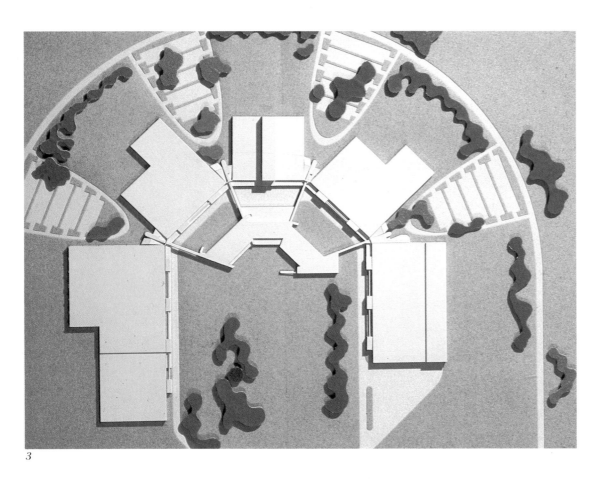

3

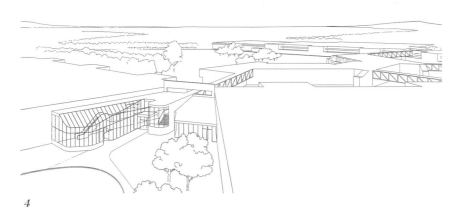

4

Third World Trade Center
New York, New York, 1978
Client: Harlem Urban Development
Corporation
with: W. Todd Springer

1 Overall view
2 Ground-floor plan
3 Model. View from southeast
4 Model. View from west
5 Longitudinal section

1

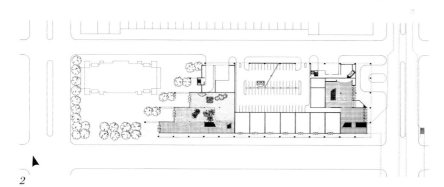

2

3

4

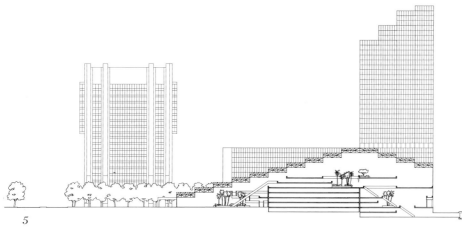

5

Morningside Campus Plan
New York, New York, 1972–87
Client: Columbia University, New York, New York

1 Avery Hall extension. Alexander Kouzmanoff Architect
2 Sherman Fairchild Center for the Life Sciences. Mitchell/Giurgola Architects
3 East Campus housing. Gwathmey Siegel Architects

4 Computer Science Building. R. M. Kliment and Frances Halsband Architects
5 Uris Hall addition. Peter L. Gluck and Partners Architects
6 Rare Book and Manuscript Library. Farrell, Bell & Lennard Architects
7 Ferris Booth Hall expansion (unbuilt). James Stewart Polshek and Partners
8 Havermeyer Extension-Chemistry Building. Davis, Brody & Associates
9 Law School addition (unbuilt). Kallmann, McKinnell and Wood Architects, Inc.

10 Schermerhorn Hall renovation. Susana Torre in association with WASA Architects and Engineers
11 Lewisohn Hall renovation. Mostoller and Wood (joint venture)
12 C. V. Starr East Asian Library. Prentice & Chan, Ohlhausen Architects
13 The Center for Career Services. Charles Boxenbaum Architect
14 Jerome Greene Hall. Robert A. M. Stern Architects
15 Chandler North project (unbuilt). James Stirling, Michael Wilford & Associates in association with WASA Architects and Engineers

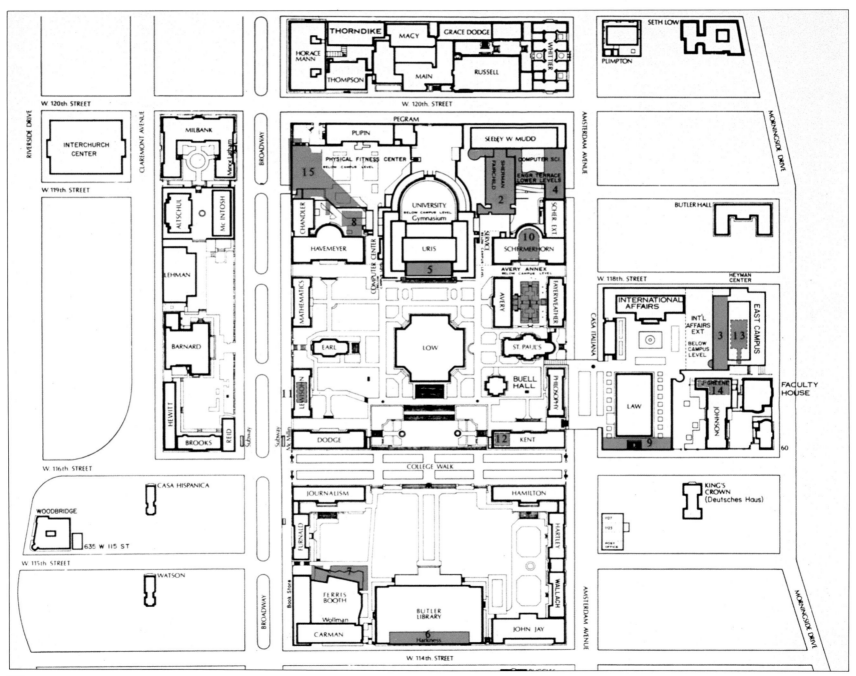

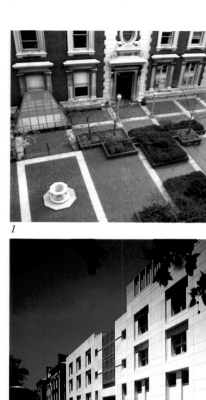

1

2

3

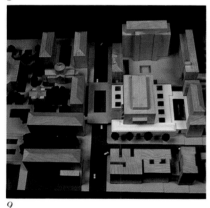

4

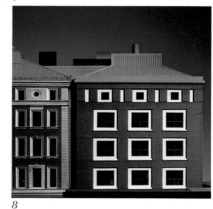

5

6

7

8

9

10

11

12

13

14

15

71

Preservation

"Preservation" as a contextual strategy concerns historic buildings whose exterior envelopes are in need of restoration, but whose interiors require significant modification. In these projects, new technologies are employed to restore the decaying historic structure or simulate its original appearance. Many restorations must conform to strict regulatory guidelines and undergo review by publicly appointed historic preservation commissions. New design is limited primarily to artifacts and assemblies, such as light fixtures, railings, signs, hardware, and marquees. In these projects the architect must coordinate a diverse team of paint restorers, material conservators, historians, tax consultants, real estate advisers, zoning lawyers, and marketing consultants, in addition to the standard technical consultants. Historic preservation projects have had a "civilizing" influence on our office. When preservationists and architects work next to one another, the emphasis on traditional craftsmanship and fine detailing affects the attitude of those working on new buildings. On a more philosophical level, such projects allow us to resist the extraordinary pressures put upon the architect by both the popular media and certain art historians to constantly invent, repeat, or copy new formal vocabularies. A Carnegie Hall, Brotherhood Synagogue, or Hall of Fame makes the office a saner and less vainglorious place to work: it de-emphasizes the individual ego involvement that unfortunately characterizes so much of what is lauded as "high-style" design these days. Today, preservation commissions serve to reinforce a continuing appreciation of the manner in which buildings are constructed, to heighten awareness of the importance of historic buildings in cities, and to encourage the development of expertise in the integration of twentieth-century technologies in eighteenth- and nineteenth-century buildings. For all of the emotional travail and bureaucratic delays that preservation projects entail, their ultimate social value, particularly in a free market economy where real estate development runs rampant and craftsmanship is fast disappearing, is inestimable.

1 *Notre Dame, Paris, France. 1163–1300*
2 *Mortuary temples of Mentuhotep and Hatshepsut, Deir el Bahari. 2050 B.C. and 1500 B.C.*
3 *Monticello, Charlottesville, Virginia. Thomas Jefferson, 1771–82*
4 *Main Street, Akron, Ohio. Circa 1960*

Oster Residence II *interior*
New York, New York, 1960
Client: Gerald and Gisela Oster

1 *View from West 11th Street*
2 *Ground-floor plan*
3 *Living/dining room*
4 *Front parlor*

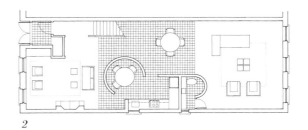

2

1

3

4

Residential Treatment Center for
Big Brothers, Inc. *renovation and interior*
New York, New York, 1966
Client: Big Brothers, Inc.
with: Walfredo Toscanini (associate architect)

1

2 *Longitudinal section*
3 *Main-floor plan*
4 *Entrance of restored nineteenth-century facade*
5 *New dining room in former morgue area*
6 *Dining room with recreation hall above*
7,8 *Covered garden court*

2

3

4

5

6

7

8

Clinton Youth and Family Center
renovation and interior; demolished
New York, New York, 1968
Client: West Side YMCA
with: Walfredo Toscanini (associate
architect), Howard Kaplan, David Bliss
(graphic designer)

1

2

1 *Main entrance*
2 *Ground-floor lobby with rediscovered vaulted*
  ceilings
3 *New gymnasium in courtroom*
4 *Play area with trompe l'oeil trees*
5 *Axonometric section*

3

4

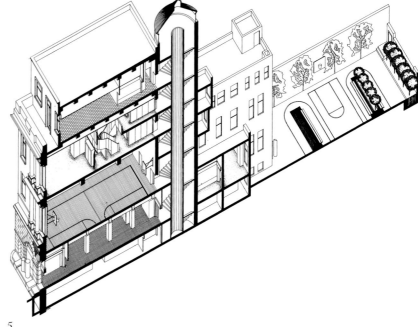

5

**Brotherhood Synagogue and Memorial
Garden** *restoration*
(Kellum and King, 1859)
New York, New York, 1974 (synagogue),
1977 (garden)
Client: Brotherhood Synagogue
with: Richard M. Olcott (garden)

1

1 Gramercy Park facade of restored Friends Meeting
  House
2 Interior of restored sanctuary
3 Ground-floor site plan
4 Three-dimensional drawing showing relationship
  of garden to building

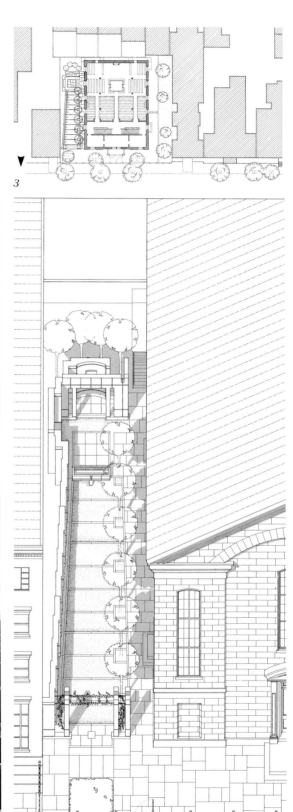

3

2

4

5

5 *Detail of Garden of Remembrance*
6 *Sketch of garden detail*

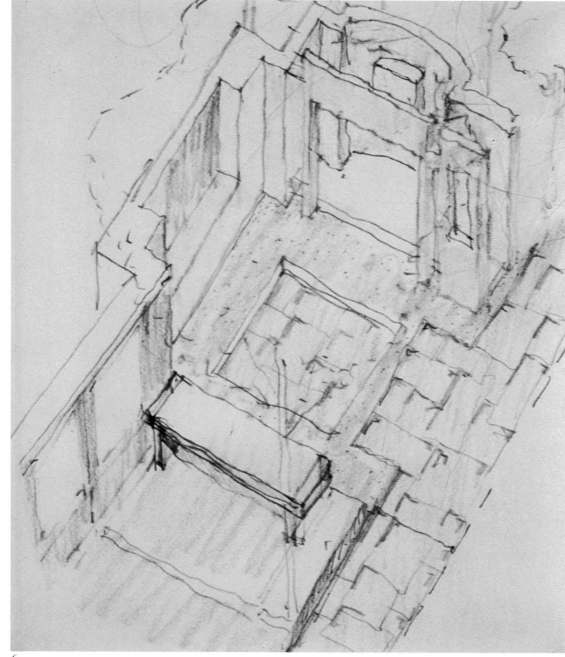

6

The Urban Center and Bookstore
(McKim, Mead, and White, 1884)
New York, New York, 1977
Client: The Municipal Art Society
with: W. Todd Springer

1 Reception foyer after renovation
2 Urban Center Bookstore
3 Ground-floor plan after renovation
4 Doris C. Freedman Gallery
5 Original interior
6 Interior before renovation

1

2

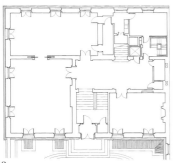

3

4

5

6

New York Society Library
renovation and interior
New York, New York, 1978
Client: New York Society Library
with: Paul S. Byard, Timothy P. Hartung,
Tyler H. Donaldson

1 *Main lobby*
2 *Ground-floor plan showing entry and stack area*
3 *Reference room*
4 *Marshall Reading Room*
5 *View from 79th Street*
6 *Longitudinal section showing reading rooms and stack area*

1

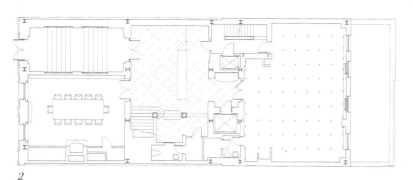

2

3

5

4

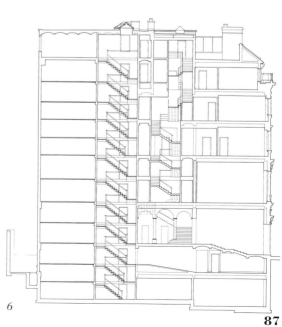

6

Carnegie Hall
New York, New York, 1978–86
Client: Carnegie Hall Corporation

Master Plan
with: Paul S. Byard, Timothy P. Hartung

Recital Hall Lobby
with: Tyler H. Donaldson

Kaplan Space
with: Joseph L. Fleischer, Tyler H.
Donaldson, Cyntha D. Thompson

Concert Hall and Lobby
with: Joseph L. Fleischer, Tyler H.
Donaldson, Gaston Silva

Weill Recital Hall
with: Joseph L. Fleischer, Tyler H.
Donaldson, Gaston Silva

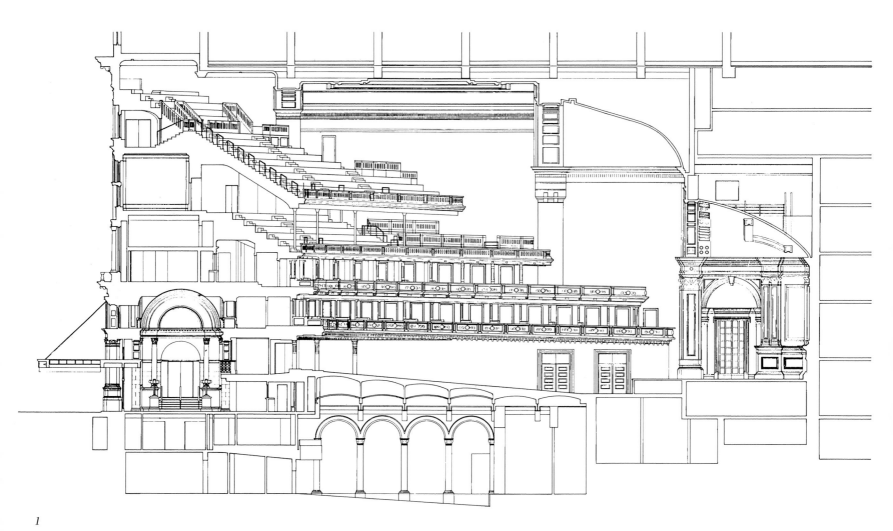

1

1 *Longitudinal section of main hall*
2 *Cutaway axonometric showing sections of Main
  Hall, Weill Recital Hall, Kaplan Space, and new
  lobby*

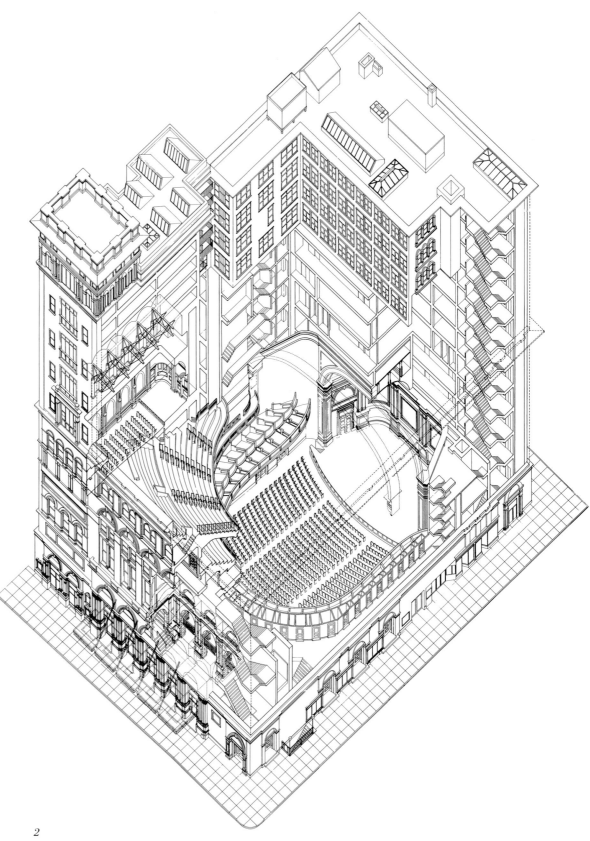

2

3 Carnegie Hall, 1891
4 New marquee
5 Old lobby
6 Longitudinal section through new lobby
7 New lobby with new light-fixtures, balconies, and
ticket booths
8 Main Hall stage with restored shell and lighting
tiara

3

4

5

6

7

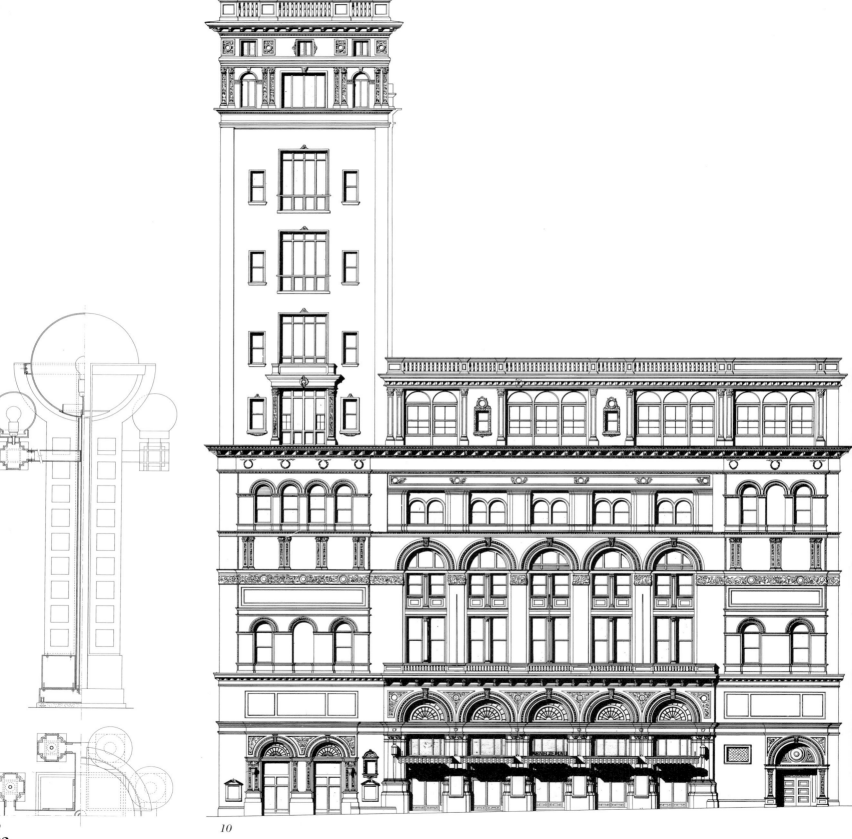

9

10

11

13

12

14

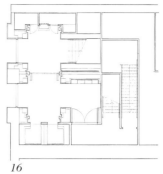

16

15

17

18

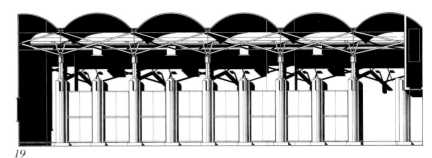

19

20

U.S. Customs House *competition*
(Cass Gilbert, 1907)
New York, New York, 1978
Client: General Services Administration
with: MBA (joint venture), Paul S. Byard,
Timothy P. Hartung

1 *Bowling Green elevation*
2 *Perspective section of rotunda and atrium courts*

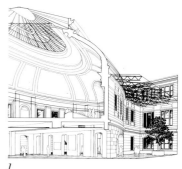

1

2

Hall of Fame *restoration*
(McKim, Mead, and White, 1892)
Bronx Community College, New York, 1979
Client: City University of New York
with: Timothy P. Hartung

1 *View of colonnade and rotunda*
2 *Ground-floor plan*

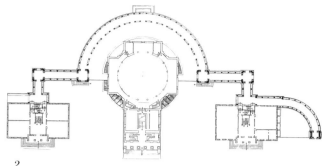

2

1

Association of the Bar of the City of New York

New York, New York, 1980
Client: Association of the Bar of the City of New York
with: Paul S. Byard, Timothy P. Hartung, Todd H. Schliemann, Gaston Silva

1

1 *New light-fixture detail*
2 *Main library*
3 *Existing facade*
4 *Proposed roof addition to south facade*
5 *Longitudinal section with addition*
6 *Stairway connecting the new reading room with the main library*
7 *Stair detail*
8 *New Bar Association reading room*

2

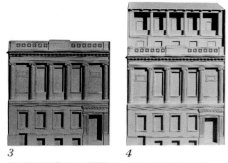

3

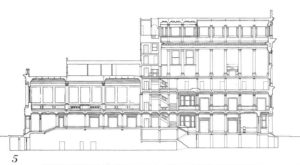

4

5

6

7

8

Stroh River Place Master Plan
Detroit, Michigan, 1983
Client: Stroh Properties, Inc.
with: Timothy P. Hartung, Richard M.
Olcott, Dan Bernstein

1

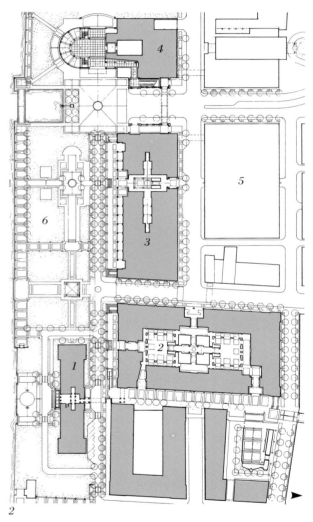

2

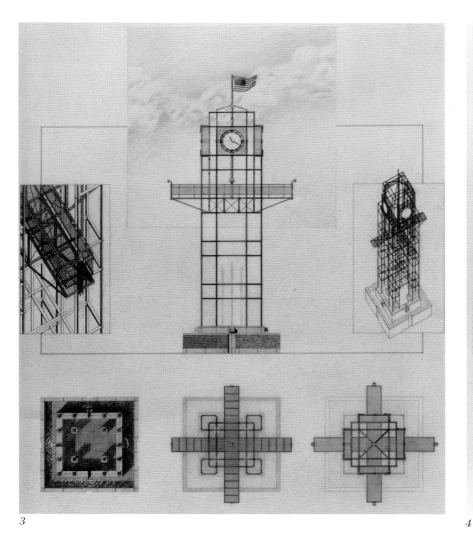

3

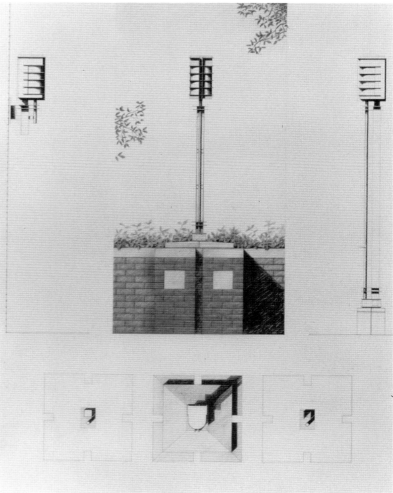

4

5 *New balustrade and light fixture*
6 *Clocktower and arrival plaza*
7 *Atrium*
8 *Atrium detail*

5

6

7

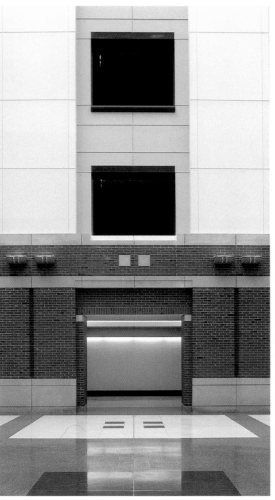

8

Grace Church School Master Plan
New York, New York, 1985
Client: Grace Church School
with: Paul S. Byard, Sara Elizabeth Caples

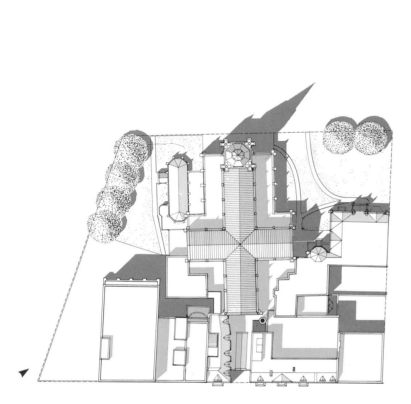

1

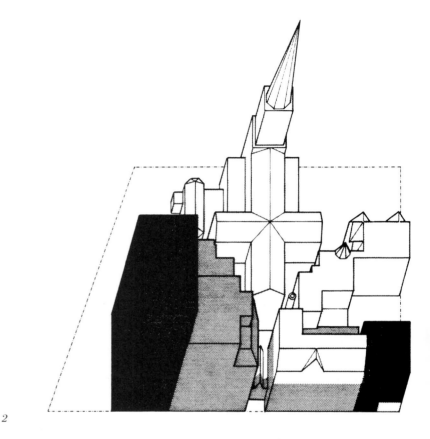

2

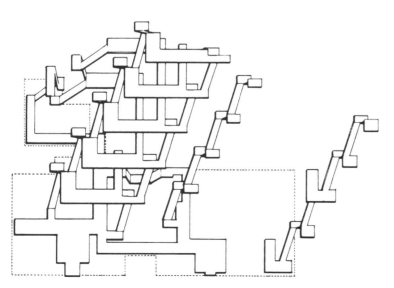

3

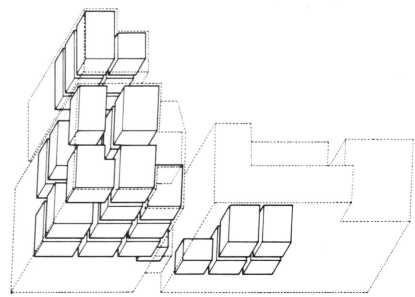

4

104

Sage Hall *renovation*
Northampton, Massachusetts, 1985
Client: Smith College
with: Paul S. Byard, Sara Elizabeth Caples

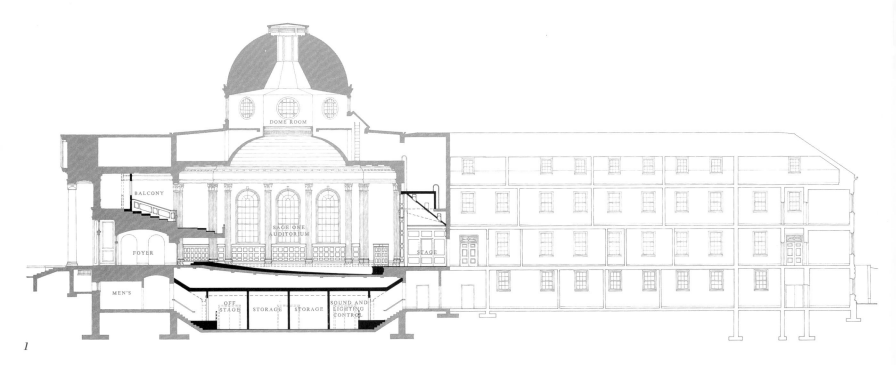

1

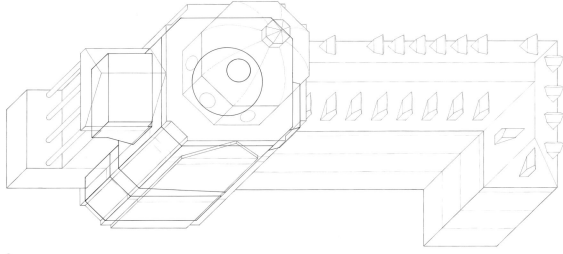

2

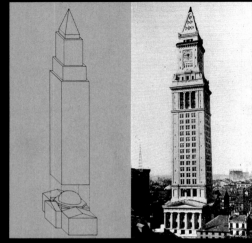

Reinforcement

"Reinforcement" comes into play when a new building program must be imposed upon an existing structure that is an integral part of the surrounding urban or suburban fabric. Compatibility of the resulting addition to the existing building thereby becomes the primary generator of the new design. Beyond the obvious concern for formal and technical integration of new and old, the primary intention is to protect a valuable, older (sometimes historic) building or complex from destruction while simultaneously reinforcing its positive qualities. Threats to an existing building of excellence often result from the increased real estate value of its site, which could eventually make it an irresistible target for destruction and replacement. The ultimate architectural objective is to use the addition as an excuse to renew an old building or group of buildings and thereby increase the historic and economic value of the new ensemble. As the value of real estate continues to rise, the conflicts between preserving architecture of quality and the creating of a new architecture—our future "landmarks"—will increase, but there is no reason that design creativity cannot coexist with a deep respect for the past.

The project that best represents this category is the New York State Bar Center in Albany, New York (1968). Nineteenth-century townhouses were both historically and physically reinforced by the new buildings behind them—which, in turn, were not compromised by requirements of literal compatability. Two ensembles, 500 Park Tower (1980) and the Metropolitan Park Tower (1985), are almost twin projects. Both are adjacent to, and partially over, historically significant buildings that occupy corner sites on major avenues. Both seek to reinforce the existing but isolated buildings, providing a context for rather than overwhelming them. The Boston Symphony Hall Master Plan (1985) calls for adding a new front to the back of the hall, extending the power of the original architecture while strengthening the location of the hall in its urban design context. The plan for the Union Theological Seminary (1986) belongs in this category because it will provide financial stability for the institution. In doing that, it will protect the integrity of the existing physical fabric while adding a new dimension to the seminary.

1 Arts Center, St. Andrews University, St. Andrews, Scotland. James Stirling Michael Wilford and Associates, 1971
2 Customs House, Boston, Massachusetts. Ammi Young, 1837–47; Tower Peabody and Stearns, 1913–15
3 Offices of the Berliner Tageblatt, Berlin, Germany. Erich Mendelsohn, 1923
4 Flatiron Building, New York. Daniel Burnham, 1902

New York State Bar Center
restoration, addition, and interior
Albany, New York, 1968
Client: New York State Bar Association
with: W. Todd Springer, Howard Kaplan

1 *Perspective section showing restored townhouses
  and new structure*
2 *Site plan*
3 *Main-floor plan*
4 *Aerial view from northeast*

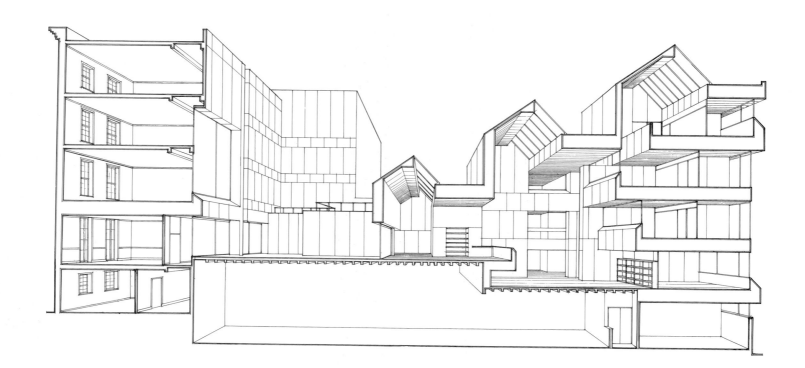

1

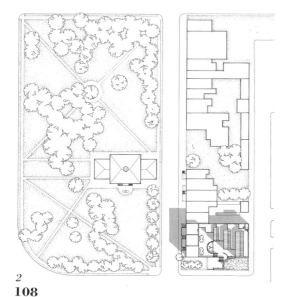

2

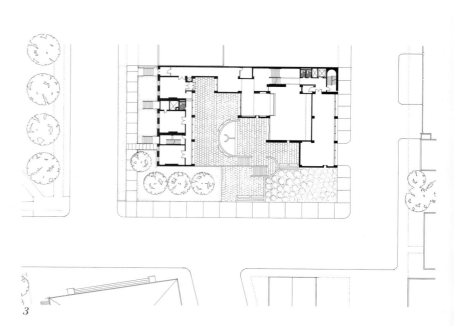

3

5 *Rear view of restored townhouses and new structure*
6 *Exterior stairs leading to upper courtyard level*
7 *Interior view of great hall looking toward Hinman Memorial Library*

5

6

7

500 Park Tower
New York, New York, 1980
Client: Equitable Life Assurance Co. of the
United States and Tishman Speyer, Inc.
with: Paul S. Byard, James G. Garrison,
Richard M. Olcott, Marla Appelbaum, Dan
Bernstein

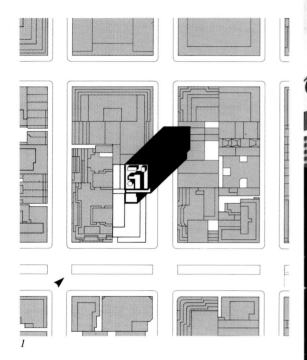

1

2

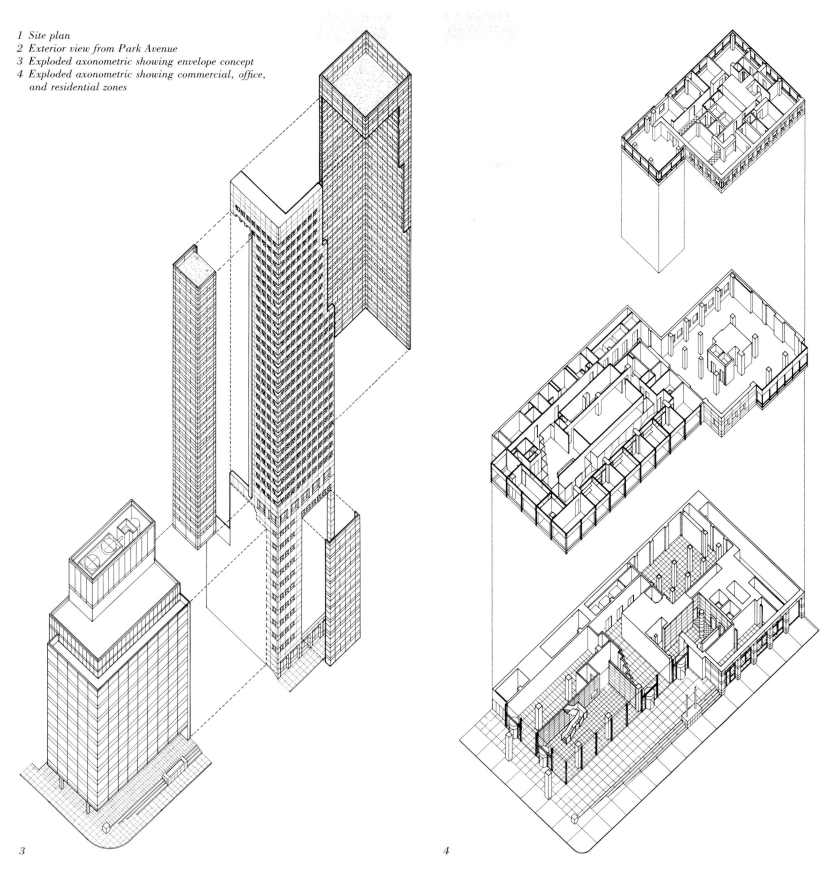

1 Site plan
2 Exterior view from Park Avenue
3 Exploded axonometric showing envelope concept
4 Exploded axonometric showing commercial, office, and residential zones

3

4

113

5

6

7

Union Theological Seminary *competition*
New York, New York, 1986
Client: General Atlantic Corporation
with: James G. Garrison, Duncan R. Hazard

1 *Section through courtyard and tower elevation*
2 *Existing seminary plan and new tower*
3 *Model. Overall view from southwest*

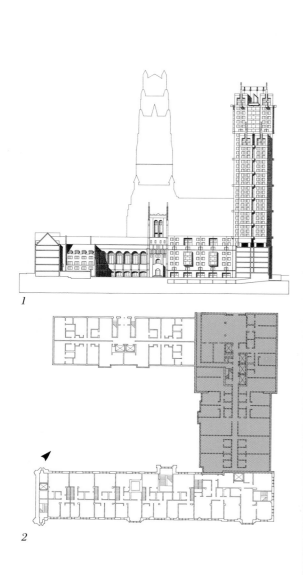

1

2

3

Boston Symphony Hall Master Plan

Boston, Massachusetts, 1985
Client: Boston Symphony Orchestra
with: Paul S. Byard, Timothy P. Hartung

1 Second-level floor plan of the expanded hall
2 Existing site plan
3 Proposed site plan
4 McKim, Mead & White Huntington Avenue
  elevation
5 Present entrance from Massachusetts Avenue

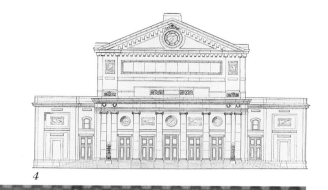

4

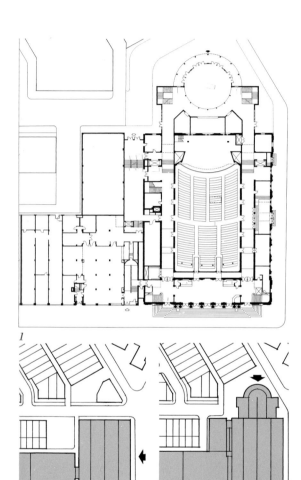

1

2

3

5

Metropolitan Park Tower
New York, New York, 1985
Client: Park Tower Realty
with: Todd H. Schliemann, Marla Appelbaum

1 Upper East Side Historic District
2 Photomontage of proposed tower as viewed from
  Central Park
3 Site plan
4,5 Exterior window details
6 South elevation
7 West elevation

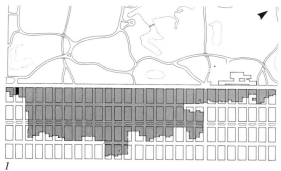

1

2

3

4

5

6

7

"Reparation" is the use of new architecture to repair poorly designed or incomplete older buildings. It involves two different categories of structures. Included in the first category are those structures of dubious or no distinction that are damaging to the urban design qualities of their surrounding area. Examples of this are college campuses (Columbia, Vassar, Harvard, etc.) whose original distinguished plans have been disfigured; or historic districts (South Street Seaport, the Upper West Side of New York, etc.) that have been eroded by urban renewal, neglect, and subsequent low-quality new development. The strategy here consists of repairing the context by screening buildings with new facades or additions and of renewing sectors of a city by the inclusion of new structures. The second category applies to disfigured existing buildings that need to be expanded, but whose sites are constrained or inadequate in size and are on or near important streets or parks where, as three-dimensional artifacts, they are part of the public domain. However, the post-war building boom created a vast quantity of inferior architecture. The absence of design regulation and community participation during these years has seriously exacerbated the situation.

The Materials Research Center at Allied Chemical Corporation (1969) began to restore the quality of the architecture in relation to the landscape and is an example of the first reparation category. The Glenfield Middle School project (1979) is an almost pure example of the second category in that the recent additions create a new rear facade and provide a presence on a public park. The difference between the Brooklyn Museum (1986) ("Completion") and this school lies primarily in the quality of the existing buildings. Both the North County Resource Recovery Facility (1982) and the IBM Headquarters Facility (1983) have much in common with Allied. In both cases a completely new architectural expression is used to envelop an undistinguished architecture. The Georg Jensen Store (1969), the Harborside Financial Center (1983), and the Emigrant Savings Bank (1984) depend upon the addition of facades to translate the buildings into public "signs." The Kingsborough Community College Health and Physical Education Building (1969) belongs in "Reparation" for a different reason. It is an example of the disposition of program elements in such a way that they conceal other parts of the building that are functionally scaleless. Finally, the New York Coliseum (1985) is rationalized by total encapsulation.

1 *Theater of Marcellus, Rome, Italy. 11 B.C.*
2 *Villa Barbaro, Maser, Italy. Andrea Palladio, 1560–68*
3 *The Opera House, Paris, France. Charles Garnier, 1874*
4 *The Piazza of St. Peter's, Rome, Italy. Gianlorenzo Bernini,
   1656–67*

Allied Chemical Materials Research Center
renovation and addition
Morristown, New Jersey, 1969
Client: Allied Chemical Corporation
with: Howard Kaplan

1

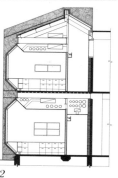

2

1 *View of the east-wing two-story addition*
2 *Section of two-story addition showing corridor*
  "zipper"
3 *Axonometric showing added wings*
4 *Interior corridor between addition and existing*
  building
5 *Director's office*

4

3

5

Kingsborough Community College
Health and Physical Education Building
Brooklyn, New York, 1969
Client: City University of New York
with: Joseph L. Fleischer, Sean W. Sculley

1 Exterior view showing administration wing, locker
  rooms, and swimming pool
2 Transverse section
3 Circulation spine exit at athletic fields
4 Ground-floor plan
5 Site plan

1

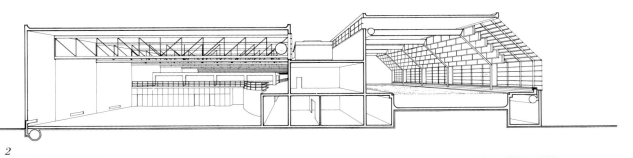

2

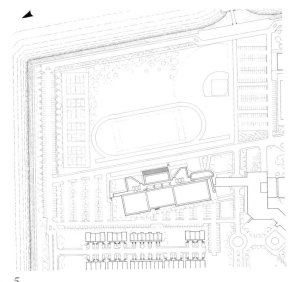

5

3

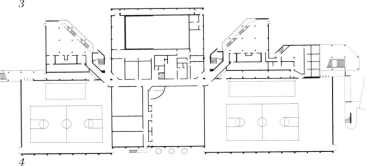

4

6

7

Georg Jensen Store *demolished*
New York, New York, 1969
Client: Georg Jensen
with: Sean W. Sculley, Joseph L. Fleischer

1 *View of interior from mezzanine*
2 *View from Madison Avenue showing restored
   building and new logo entablature*

1

2

Glenfield Middle School *renovation and addition*
Montclair, New Jersey, 1979
Client: Montclair Board of Education
with: Joseph L. Fleischer, James G. Garrison,
Timothy P. Hartung, Joanne Sliker

1 *Three-dimensional view of*
  1 new gymnasium
  2 planetarium
  3 library
  4 theater
  5 new classroom wing
2 *Main-floor plan and site plan showing new*
  facilities around raised courtyard

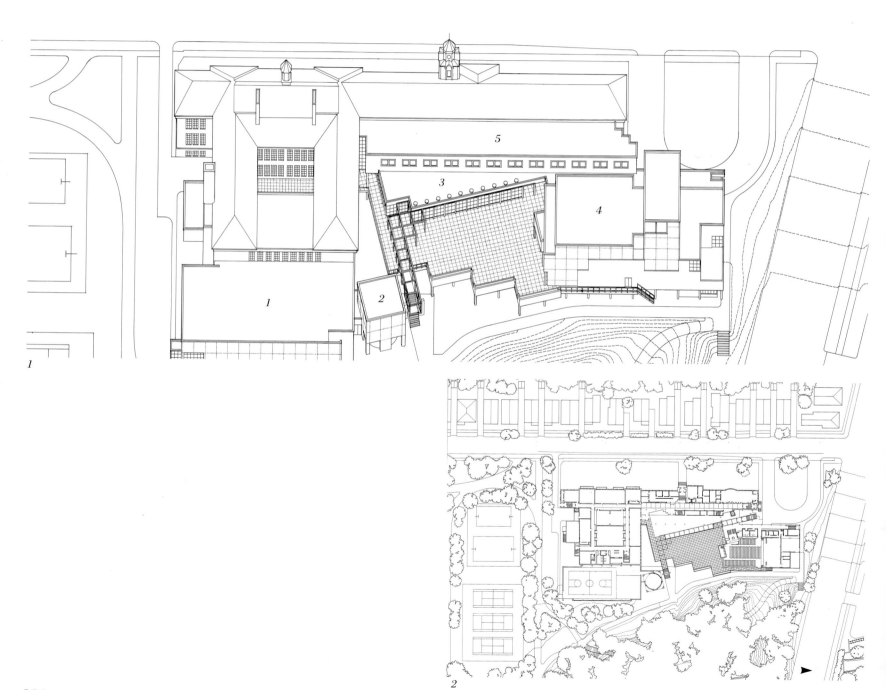

3 *Southeast elevation*
4 *East elevation showing new and old entrances*
5 *Longitudinal section through gymnasium,*
  planetarium, and theater
6 *Cross section through original school building and*
  new addition

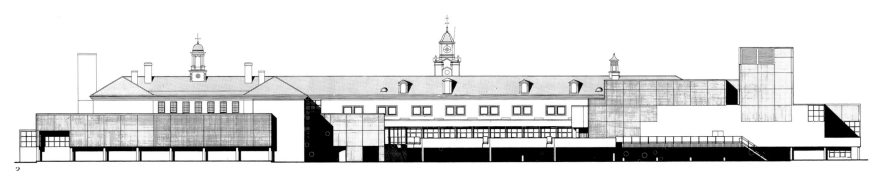

3

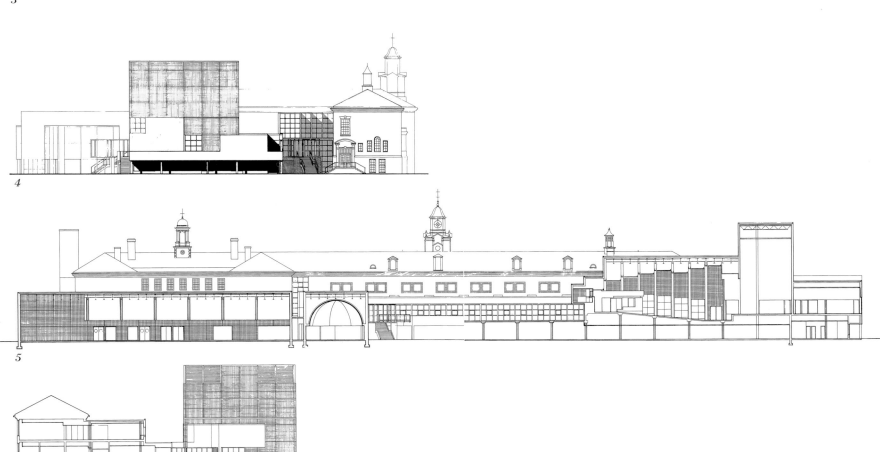

4

5

6

129

7 *View of new entry to theater, parking and service*
  level, and community room
8 *Main corridor/gallery*
9,10 *Facade details*

8

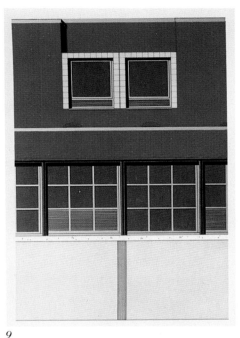

9

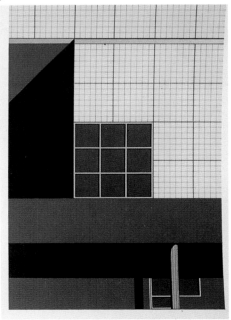

10

North County Resource Recovery Facility
San Marcos, California, 1982
Client: North County Resource Recovery
Associates
with: Paul S. Byard, Richard M. Olcott, Sara
Elizabeth Caples

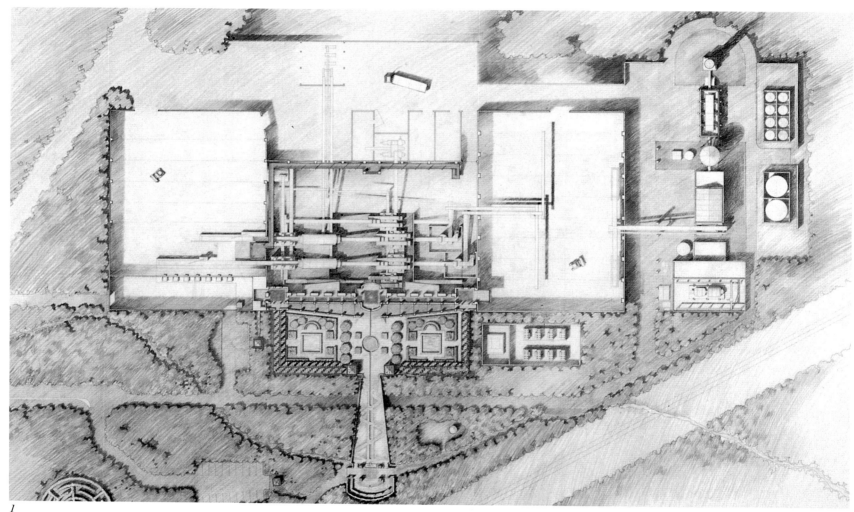

1

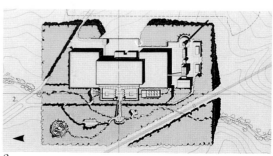

2

3

133

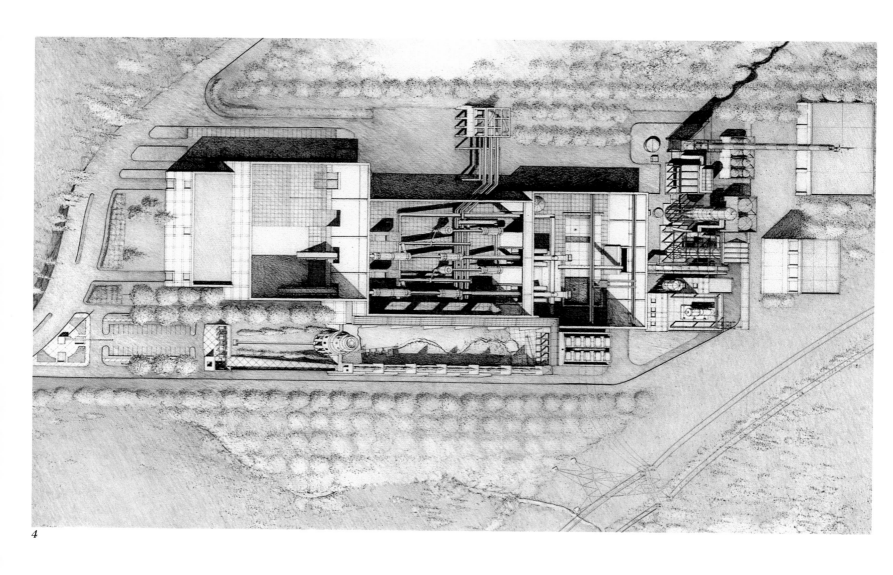

4

4 *Scheme II. Three-dimensional drawing showing*
   processing area and garden
5 *Scheme III. Entrance walkway to "trash" museum*
6 *Scheme III. View of garden trellis and viewing*
   platform
7 *Scheme III. Study of viewing platform*

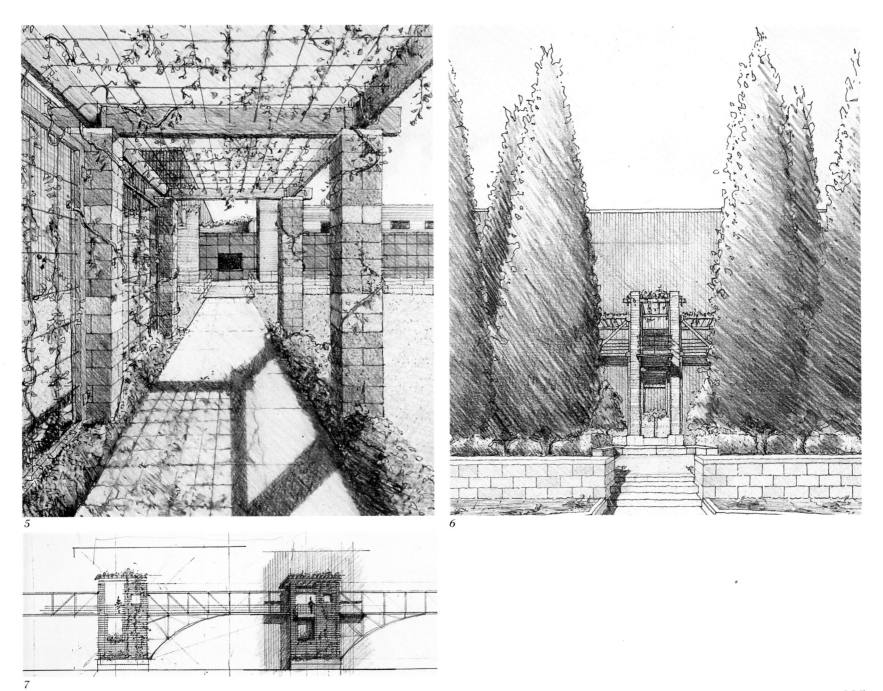

5

6

7

IBM Headquarters Facility
White Plains, New York, 1983
Client: IBM, New York, New York
with: Joseph L. Fleischer, Tyler H.
Donaldson, Duncan R. Hazard, Charmian
Place (interior designer)

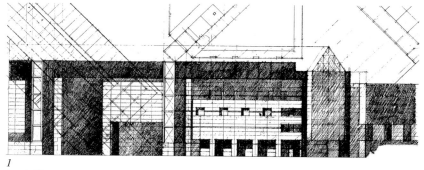

1

2

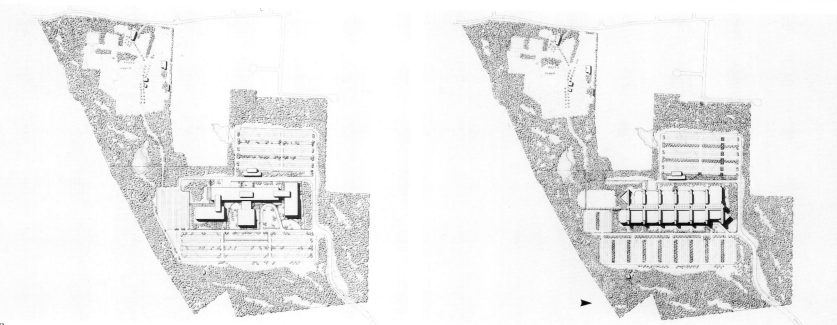

3

4

5

6

7

Harborside Financial Center *renovation*
Jersey City, New Jersey, 1983
Client: The Harborside Corporation
with: Joseph L. Fleischer, James G.
Garrison, Sara Elizabeth Caples, James R.
Gainfort

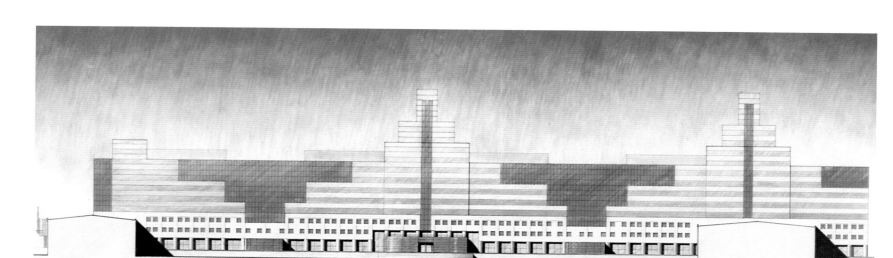

1

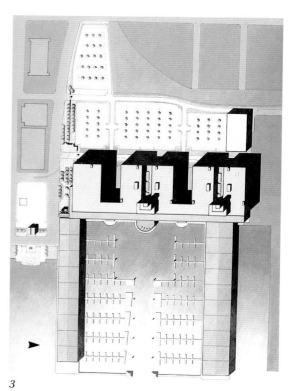

2

3

1 New east facade on Hudson River
2 Aerial view
3 Site plan
4,5,6 Entry pavilion

4

6

5

139

Emigrant Savings Bank *renovation*
New York, New York, 1984
Client: Emigrant Savings Bank
with: Todd H. Schliemann

1

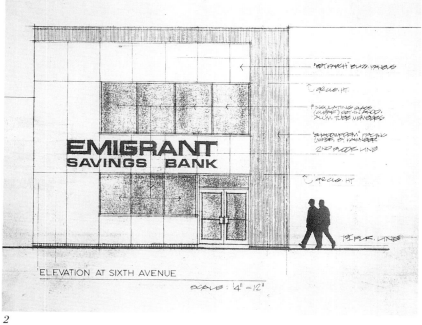

2

3

1 *Existing facade*
2 *First design by bank architect*
3 *Sketch of new facade design*
4,5 *Proportional elevation studies*
6 *Completed facade*
7 *Facade detail*

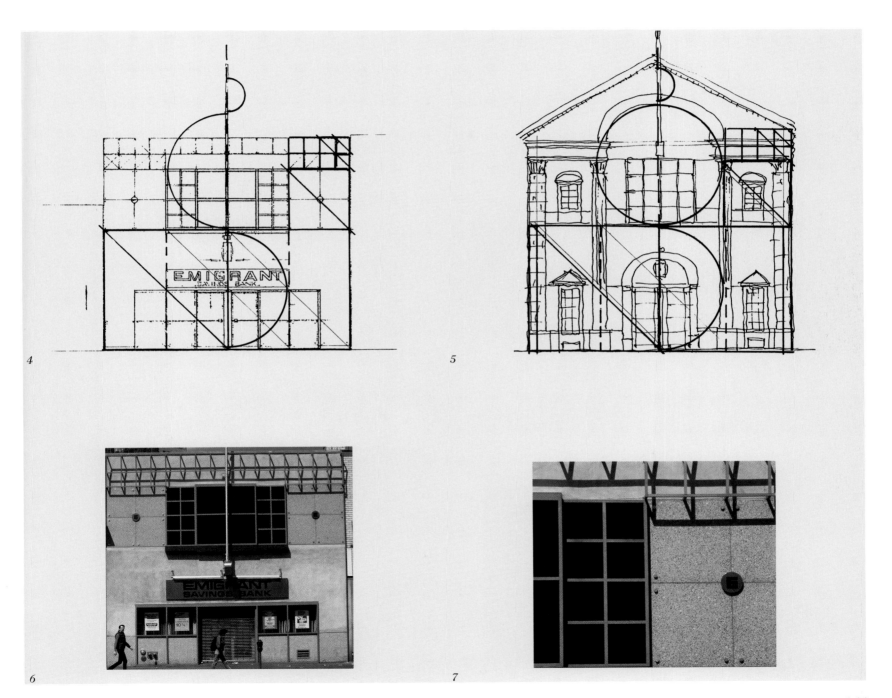

4

5

6

7

New York Coliseum Competition
New York, New York, 1985
Client: Hirschfeld Realty
with: Todd H. Schliemann, Dan Bernstein

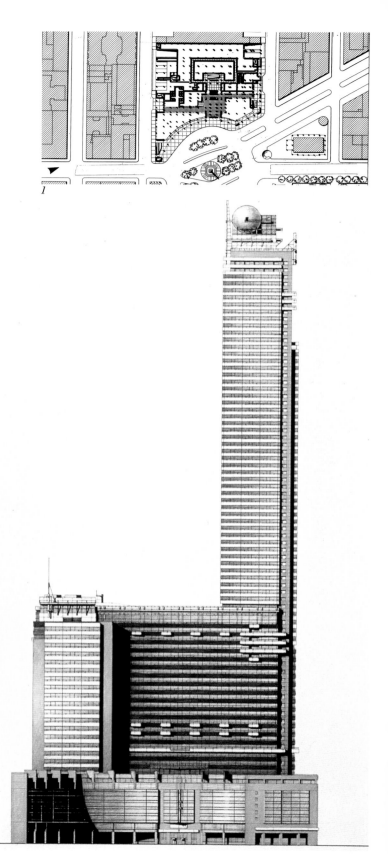

2

3

1 Ground-floor and site plan
2 North elevation
3 East elevation
4 Detail of "moon" at top of building
5 Night view

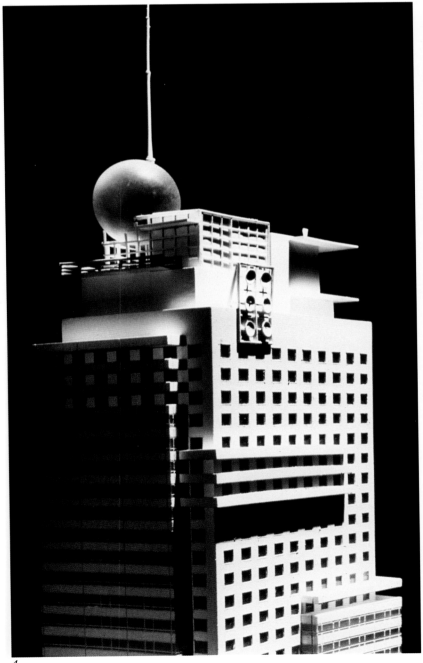

4

5

"Conservation" is a strategy for using architecture to protect or reinforce natural landscape features. Solutions involve placing the building so that it achieves some or all of the following goals: the halting or forestalling of modifications to the landscape; the preservation of views; the maintenance of the visual integrity of an important piece of property; or the stabilization of a historic precinct.

Two pure examples of this strategy are the Quinco Mental Health Center (1969), which welds the sides of a creek together, and, in so doing, protects existing natural features, and the Bronfman Pool Pavilion (1969), which emphasizes the importance of topographic manipulation. Choate-Rosemary Hall (1969) preserves its beautiful natural setting by being woven into the topography and surrounding woods, while the Loft's Pond Park Pavilion (1965) almost "grows" out of the landscape. The work at the Delafield Estates (1979) reestablishes the pre-existing, formal, man-made landscape geometries, and restores the existing wetlands and specimen trees from destruction by the careful placement of its component buildings. The Trancas Medical Center (1977) "conserves" by making invisible the vast parking lots that would normally surround it. And the Princeton Nurseries project (1986) accommodates the pre-existing natural landscape features by its overall plan.

1 *Spanish cave houses, near Malaga, Spain*
2 *Ise Shrine, Honshu, Japan: third century*
3 *The château of Chenonceaux, Chenonceaux, France, 1515;*
   Bridge, Philibert de l'Orme, 1555–59; Gallery, Jean Bullant, 1576
4 *Taliesen West, Scottsdale, Arizona. Frank Lloyd Wright, 1938*

Loft's Pond Park Pavilion
Baldwin, Long Island, 1965
Client: Baldwin Parks Recreation Department
with: Sean W. Sculley

1 *View of pavilion from park*
2 *Site plan showing pavilion, terraces, and pond*

1

2

146

Bronfman Recreation Pavilion
Purchase, New York, 1969
Client: Mr. and Mrs. Edgar Bronfman

1

2

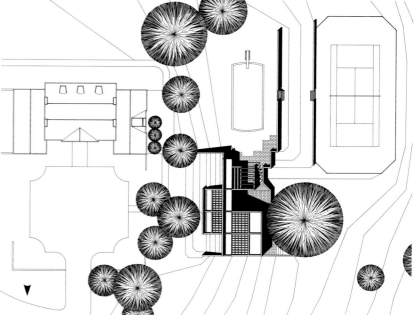

3

148

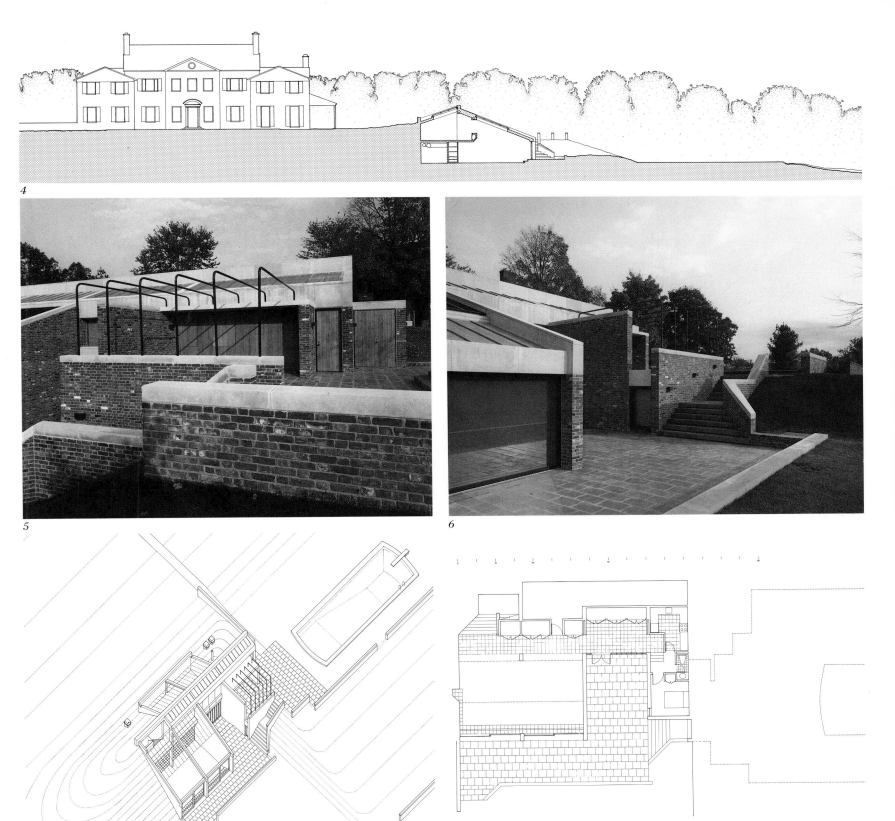

4

5

6

7

8

149

Quinco Mental Health Center
Columbus, Indiana, 1969
Client: Region 10 Foundation
with: W. Todd Springer, Dimitri Linard,
James McCullar

2

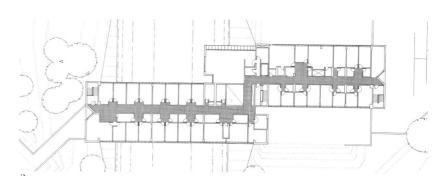

3

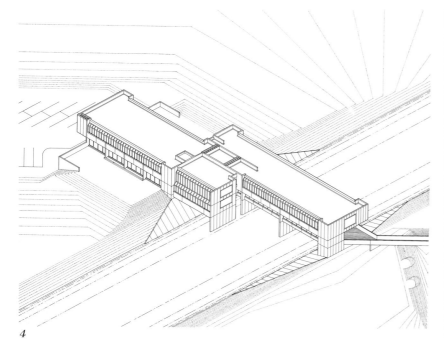

4

6

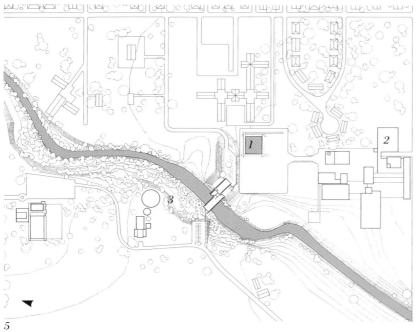

5

7

Choate-Rosemary Hall Campus
Wallingford, Connecticut, 1969
Client: Choate-Rosemary Hall
with: W. Todd Springer, Pamela Babey
(interior designer)

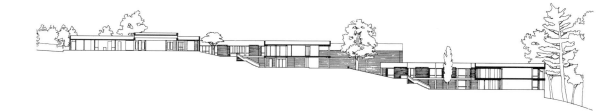

2

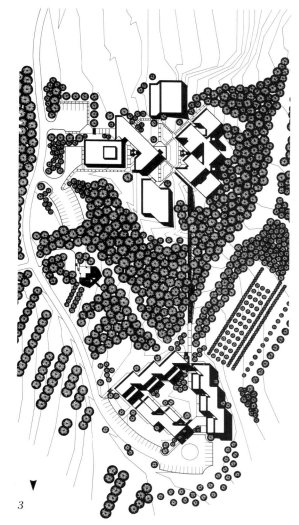

3

4

5

Trancas Medical Center
Napa, California, 1977
Client: Trancas Associates
with: Peter L. Gluck and Associates (joint venture), Joseph L. Fleischer, James G. Garrison, Marla Appelbaum

1 Site plan
2 View of entrance from upper parking area
3 Aerial view of new complex
4 Internal vehicular entry showing parking under building and pedestrian bridge
5 Building elevation
6 View of public corridor, waiting rooms, and opposite wing
7 Classroom, upper level
8 Axonometric view

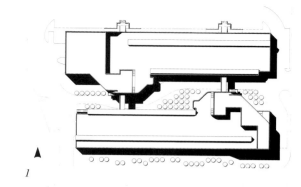

1

2

3

4

156

5

6

7

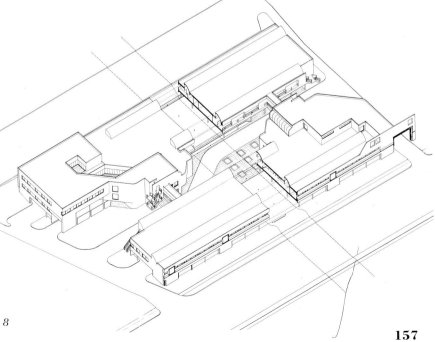

8

Princeton Nurseries *project*
Plainsborough and South Brunswick,
New Jersey, 1986
Client: Laramie-Dawson Corp.
with: James G. Garrison, Susan Rodriguez

1

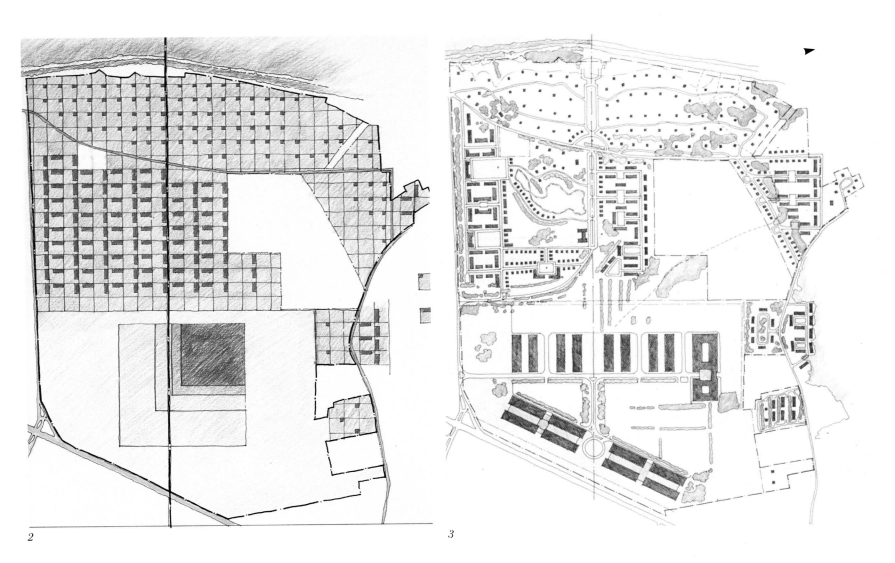

1 Sketches of housing types
2 Density analysis for residential and office areas
3 Final site plan

2

3

159

Delafield Estates

Riverdale, New York, 1979
Client: Delafield Estates, Ltd.
Scheme I with: Peter L. Gluck and
Associates (joint venture), Tyler H. Donaldson
Scheme II with: Timothy P. Hartung, Todd
H. Schliemann

2

1 Rendering of cul-de-sac house
2 Aerial view showing existing manor house and
  new units
3 Elevation through site showing three unit types
4 Plans of three units shown in elevation

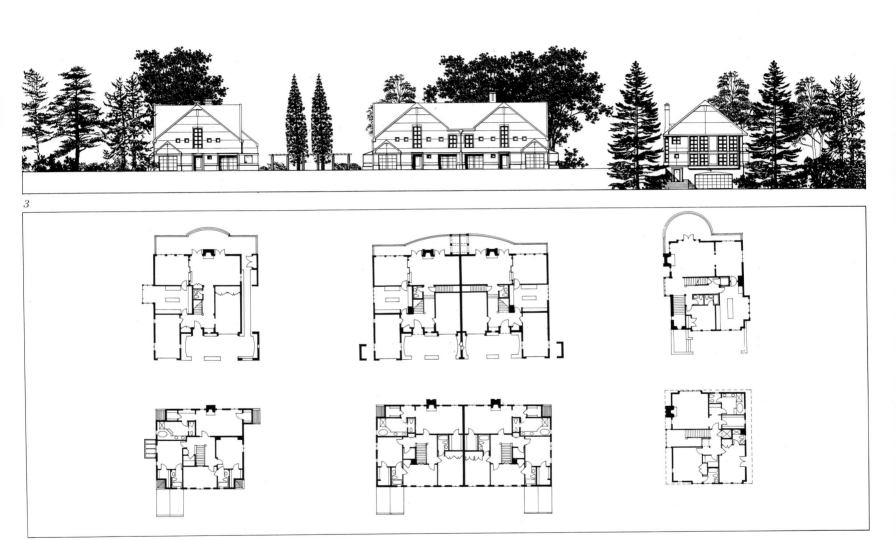

3

4

161

Completion

"Completion" resolves two distinct conditions. The first is the replacement of the "missing tooth"—the gap in the street wall or the eroded corner. This contextual strategy is often complicated by the fact that such conditions occur in older neighborhoods that are either statutory or de facto historic districts. The second condition applies to new precincts where the creative accommodation of urban design guidelines defines the volumes and expressions of the architecture. The destruction and rebuilding of cities goes on indefinitely. And, although the polemics of both the appointed and self-appointed guardians of our urban patrimony delay and constrain the process of re-building, the ultimate result can be powerful and profoundly humanizing.

The Washington Court project (1984) completes a corner and fills a gap (formerly a parking lot) in a historic neighborhood. The Eighth Avenue Residential Condominium (1985) similarly completes a block that had been eroded over time. The accommodation of design guidelines is represented by Liberty House (1982) at Battery Park City. The Brooklyn Museum (1985; master plan) is completed by a new southern facade composed of new functional program elements, and the Barnard College Student Residence (1985) finishes a quadrangle and begins to make rational once again the overall design of an urban campus. The U.S. Consulate and

Residence in Lyons (1978) and the Wesleyan University Student Center (1969) fill in open sites that have disrupted the urbanistic integrity of their immediate surroundings. The Rochester Riverside Convention Center (1980) parallels these last two projects by the way it unites the river and Main Street and also, like Kingsborough, "repairs" by concealing the blank walled volumes of its exhibit halls. The other projects in this section similarly complete and rationalize their less than optimal original settings.

---

1 Yale University Art Gallery, New Haven, Connecticut. Louis I. Kahn, 1953
2 Alexanderplatz project collage, Berlin, Germany. Ludwig Mies van der Rohe, 1928
3 Campidoglio, Rome, Italy. Michelangelo, 1538–1600
4 Karl Marx-Hof, Vienna, Austria. Karl Ehn, 1927

Bedford-Stuyvesant Community Center
Brooklyn, New York, 1967
Client: Bedford-Stuyvesant Residential Corp.
with: Joseph L. Fleischer

1 Model showing ramp to galleria over street
2 Street-level site plan showing relationship of
cultural and recreational buildings

1

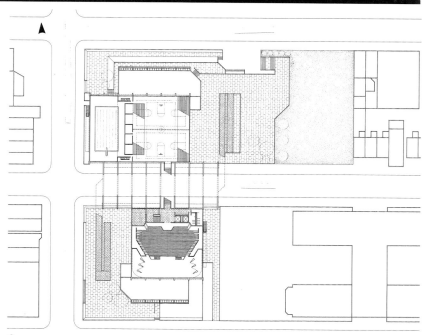

2

164

Wesleyan University Student Center and Central Plant

Middletown, Connecticut, 1969
Client: Wesleyan University
with: Joseph L. Fleischer, W. Todd Springer,
Carl Berger

1 Section showing relationship to existing
  brownstone row and underground boiler plant
2 Axonometric of elevations facing town
3 Ground-floor plan

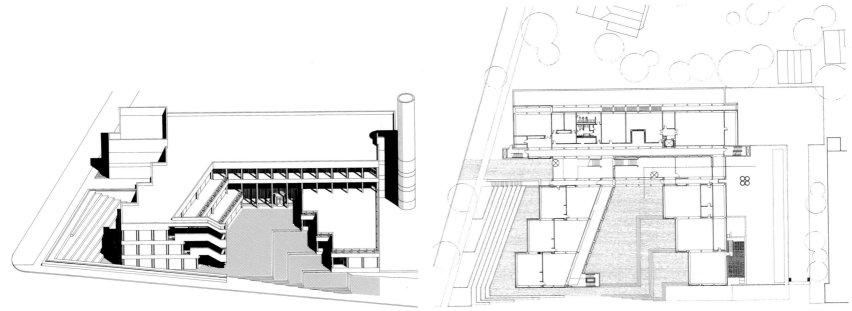

1

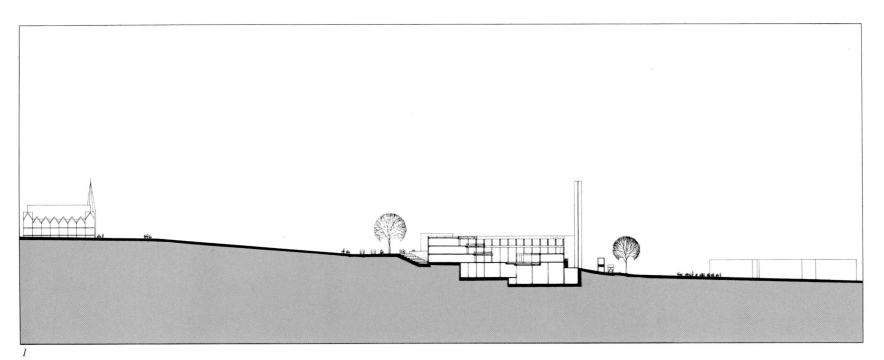

2

3

Twin Parks East Housing
Bronx, New York, 1969
Client: New York State Urban Development
Corporation, Albany, New York
with: Joseph L. Fleischer, Michael Herlands

1

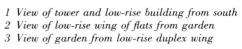
1 View of tower and low-rise building from south
2 View of low-rise wing of flats from garden
3 View of garden from low-rise duplex wing

2

3

5   6

4

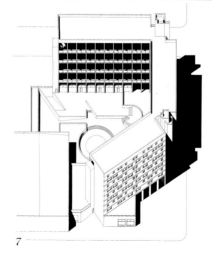
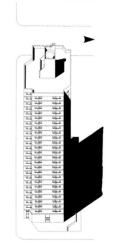

7

Intermediate School 172
New York, New York, 1973
Client: New York City Board of Education
with: W. Todd Springer, Joseph L. Fleischer

1 *View of model over Amsterdam Avenue showing*
  three "houses" on Highbridge Park
2 *Site plan*

1

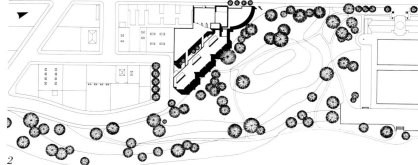

170

2

U.S. Consulate and Residence: Lyons
Lyons, France, 1978
Client: U.S. Department of State,
Washington, D.C.
with: Paul S. Byard, James G. Garrison

1 View from garden of chancery and ambassador
  residence
2 Ground-floor and site plans showing relationship
  to boulevard and park

1

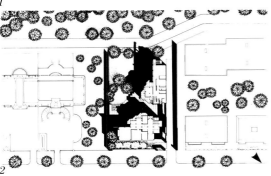

2

Rochester Riverside Convention Center

Rochester, New York, 1980
Client: City of Rochester
with: Joseph L. Fleischer, James G.
Garrison, Sara Elizabeth Caples, James R.
Gainfort

1 West elevation as seen from the Genesee River
2 Cross section through service wing, exhibition hall, galleria, and riverside plaza
3 Site plan
4 Exhibition hall floor plan
5 Axonometric of construction systems

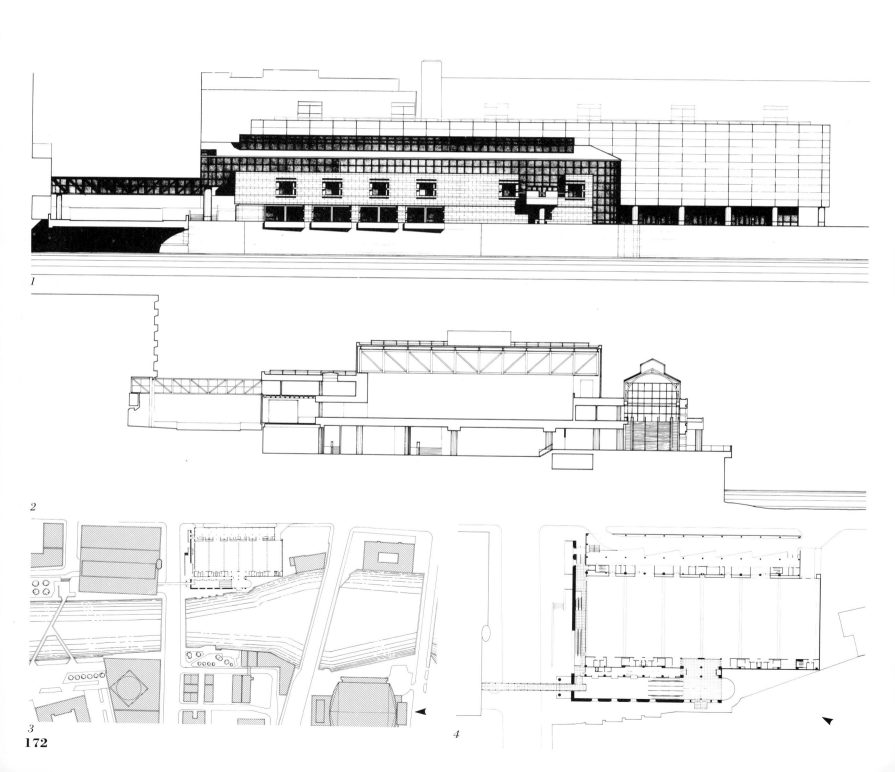

6 *Main entrance and pedestrian bridge, looking southeast*
7 *View of galleria and terrace overlooking Genesee River*
8 *View of galleria from Genesee River*
9 *Interior view of galleria toward main entrance*

6

7

8

Liberty House
New York, New York, 1982
Client: Mariners Cove Associates
with: Todd H. Schliemann,
Sara Elizabeth Caples

1 *View from south of Liberty House on*
  esplanade
2 *Aerial view*
3 *Drawing of entrance canopy*
4 *Site plan*

1

3

4

2

177

Washington Court
New York, New York, 1984
Client: Philips International Holding Corp.
with: James G. Garrison, Gaston Silva

1 Sixth Avenue facade
2 Facade through canopy
3 Entry
4 Duplex interior

1

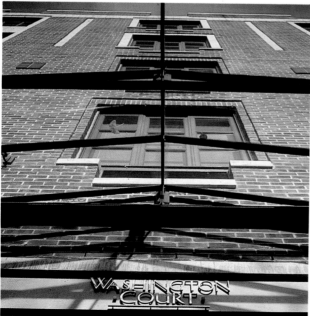

2

3

4

5

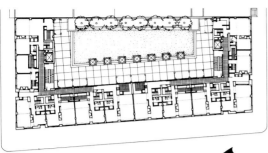

7

6

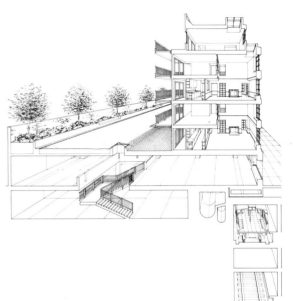

8

Eighth Avenue Residential Condominium
New York, New York, 1985
Client: Philips International Holding Corp.,
New York, New York
with: James G. Garrison

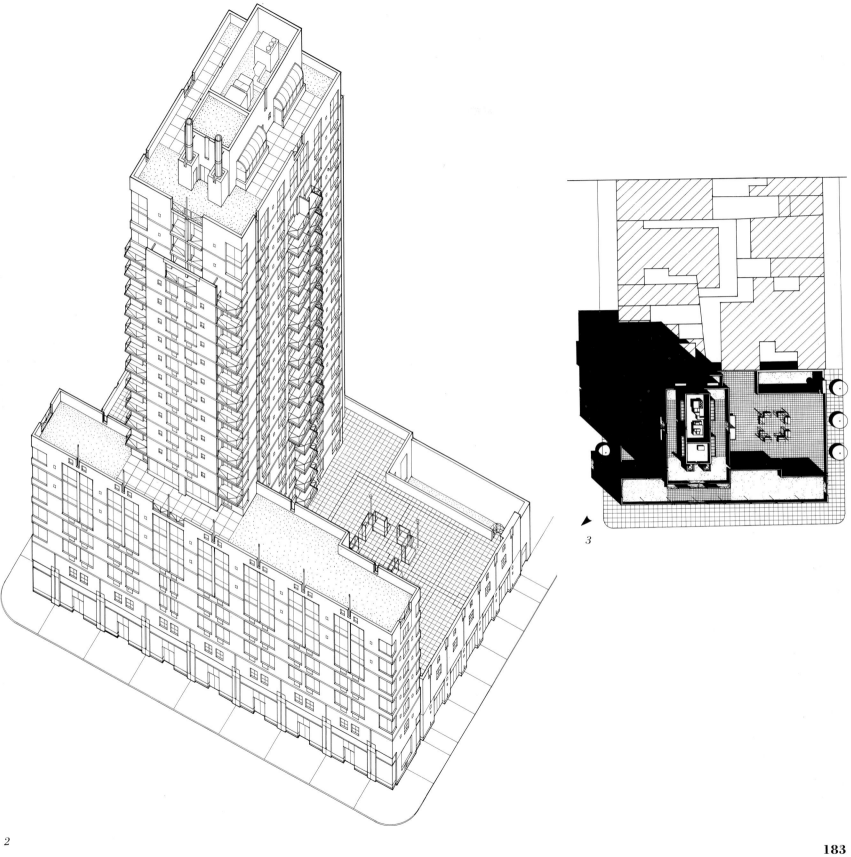

2

▶
3

Paris Opera Competition
Paris, France, 1983
Client: City of Paris
with: Richard M. Olcott

1 *Rue de Lyon elevation*
2 *Axonometric of proposed complex*
3 *Place de la Bastille elevation and theater section*

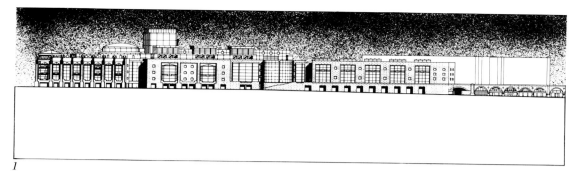

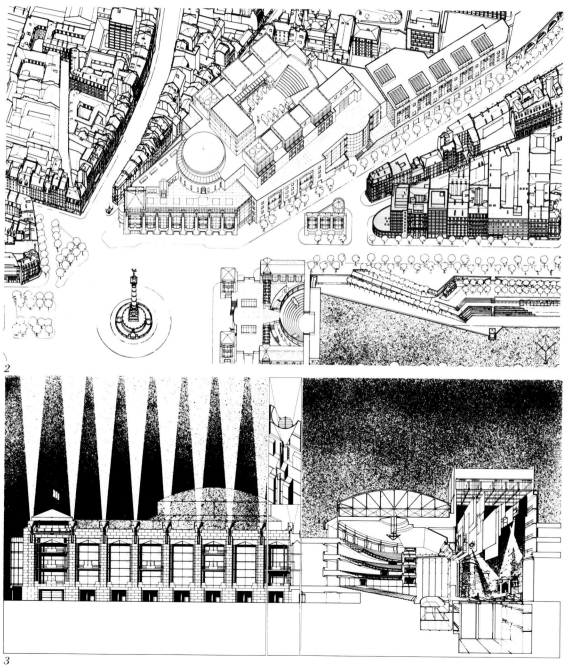

Bard College Student Residence

Annandale-on-Hudson, New York,
New York, 1985
Client: Bard College
with: James G. Garrison, Timothy P. Hartung

1 *Ground-floor plan*
2 *Perspective of complex*
3 *Facade detail*
4 *Axonometric showing relationship of new and existing dormitories*

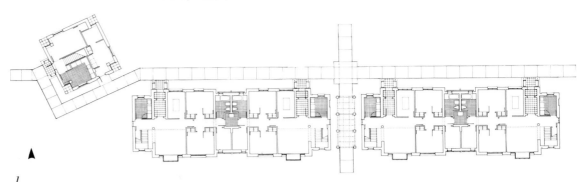

1

2

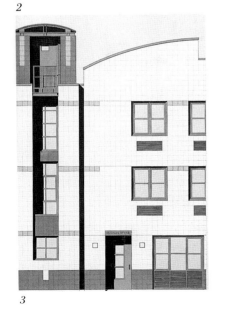

3

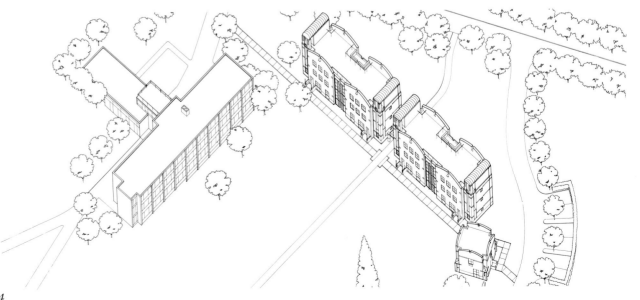

4

Bronxville West
Bronxville, New York, 1985
Client: Bronxville West Realty Partners,
New Rochelle, New York
with: Todd H. Schliemann, Marla Appelbaum

1 Inner courtyard
2 Perspective of Parkway Road and Palmer Avenue
  intersection
3 Perspective of main entrance gateway
4 Facade detail
5 Site plan showing five "houses" around courtyard
6 Cross section
7,8 Bronxville existing context

1

2

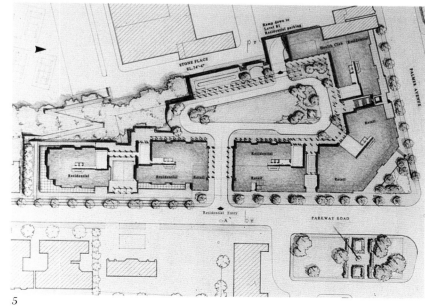

5

186

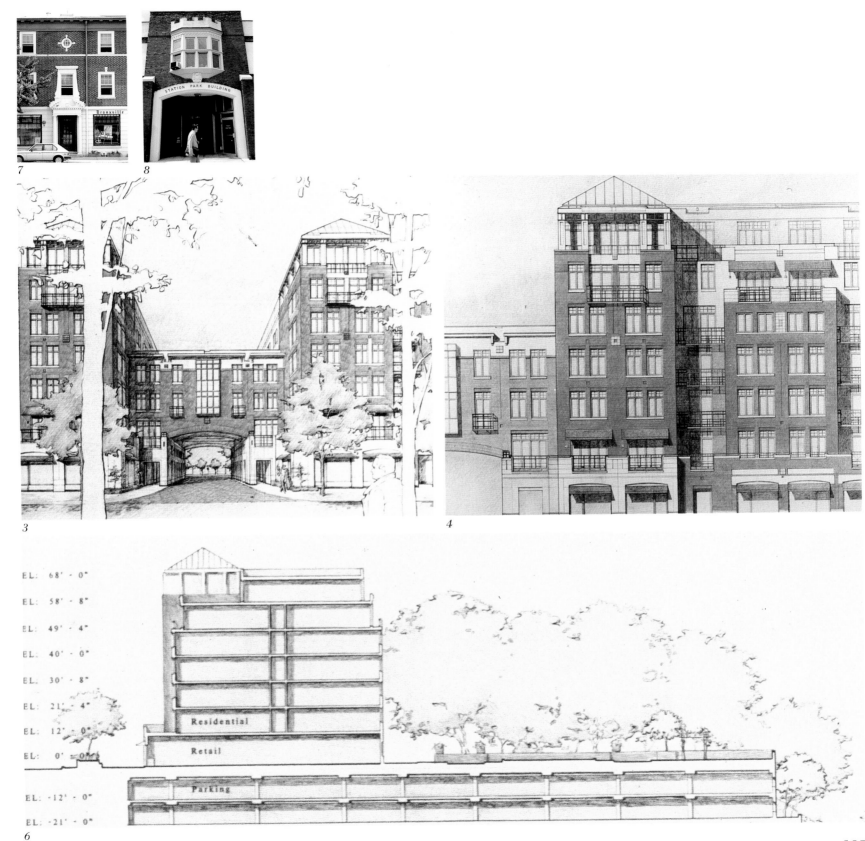

7

8

3

4

EL: 68' - 0"

EL: 58' - 8"

EL: 49' - 4"

EL: 40' - 0"

EL: 30' - 8"

EL: 21' - 4"

EL: 12' - 0"   Residential

EL: 0' - 0"   Retail

EL: -12' - 0"   Parking

EL: -21' - 0"

6

Barnard College Student Residence
New York, New York, 1985
Client: Barnard College
with: Joseph L. Fleischer, Richard M.
Olcott, Duncan R. Hazard, Joanne Sliker,
Jihyon Kim

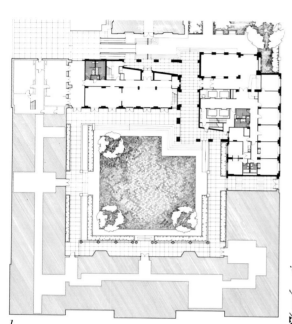

1

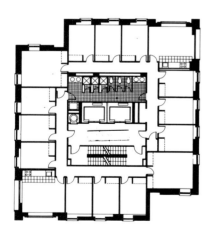

2

3

1 Ground-floor plan showing completion of
quadrangle
2 Tower-floor plan
3 Perspective south from Broadway
4 Campus master plan
5 North elevation tower detail

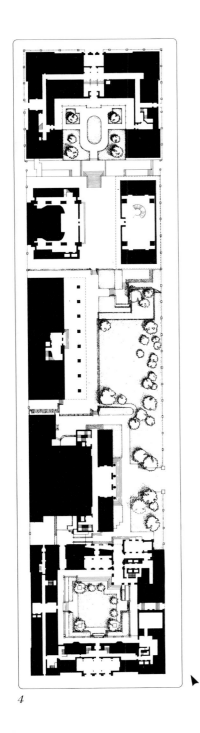

4

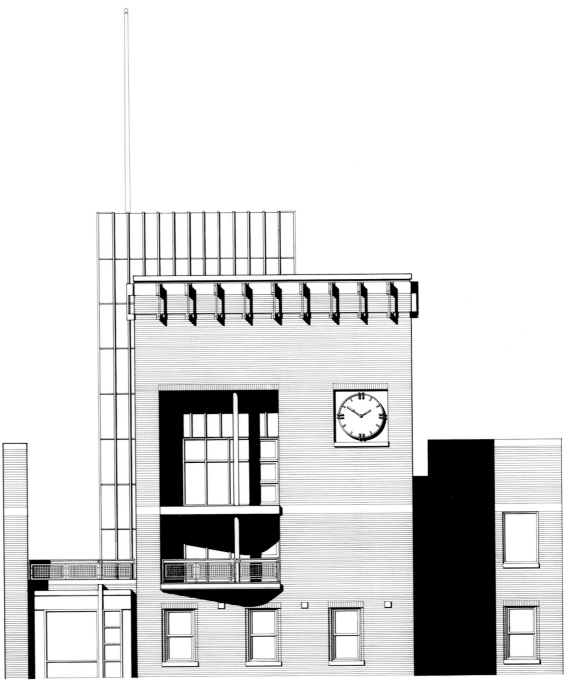

5

189

Brooklyn Museum Master Plan
competition
Brooklyn, New York, 1985
Client: Brooklyn Museum
with: Arata Isozaki and Associates (joint venture), James G. Garrison, Duncan R. Hazard

1 Site plan
2 Aerial view of model showing new south facade
3 Cross section through proposed addition
4 Existing Eastern Parkway facade
5 The Brooklyn Museum 1895 plan and built portion
6 The Brooklyn Museum 1987 piano nobile plan

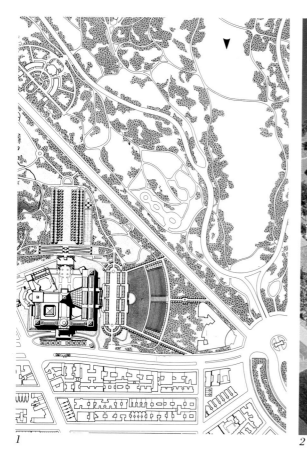

1

2

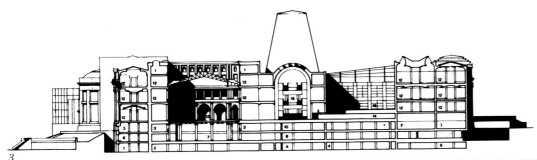

3

4

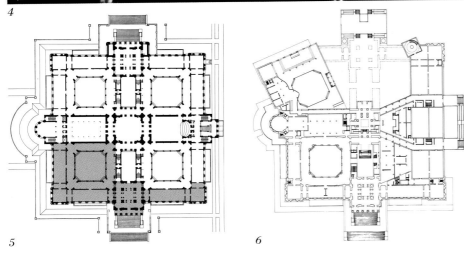

5

6

The term "creation" refers to situations in which there exists neither a man-made nor a significant natural context from which a central architectural idea for a building can be generated. Here, one is faced with complex programs and few, if any, natural or urban contextual limitations on the design of the building. In such cases the building must become its own context. Design solutions are required that are particularly rich in tectonic and spatial invention, both internally and externally, in order to substitute for such missing surroundings as familiar views, a historic setting, fragments of existing buildings, or a rich natural landscape.

The U.S. Embassy in Oman (1984) is in a desert at the edge of the sea, while the Teijin laboratories (1963 and 1964) are located in industrial "deserts." Like historic town plans, both create exceedingly complex internal pedestrian circulation routes that use courtyards, interior "plazas," asymmetrical "streets," and limited vistas. Oster Residence I (1957) and the Donovan Pool House (1967) are freestanding objects although both relate strongly to their natural settings. The Service Groups (1968), the Physical Education Building at Old Westbury (1975), the York College Theater (1985), the Peak Competition (1984), the Englewood Public Works Facility (1973), and the Hudson Valley Festival of the Arts (1985) are all dependent upon the machine as metaphor, indicating their functions by volumet-ric expressions with their structure and/or cladding employed to emphasize their independence from their surroundings. The Harlem Shopping Mall (1978) and the Con Ed West Side Operations Center (1978), although in dense urban situations, have been consciously designed as object buildings for symbolic purposes—as public signs of renewal. Finally, the Atlantic Terminal Public Housing (1971) (unlike Twin Parks East Housing [1969], which is an infill project) was built in a cleared urban renewal area and with the same need to express the ideas of urban rebirth.

1 Dr. Edith Farnsworth House, Plano, Illinois. Ludwig Mies van der Rohe, 1950
2 Unité d'habitation, Marseilles, France. Le Corbusier, 1952
3 Katsura Imperial Villa, Kyoto, Japan. Kobori Enshū, 1636
4 Fallingwater (Edgar J. Kaufmann House), Bear Run, Pennsylvania Frank Lloyd Wright, 1935

Oster Residence I
Stony Point, New York, 1957
Client: Gerald and Gisela Oster
with: Ludovica Schniewind, Associate
Architect

1

1 *View of house from south showing stone entry
   platforms*
2 *Living area with fireplace/furnace room "island"*
3 *Floor plan*

2

3

195

Teijin Central Research Institute

Tokyo, Japan, 1963
Client: Teijin Limited, Tokyo, Japan
with: Kajima Construction Corporation Design
Department

1 Site plan
2 Aerial view of new building from north
3 View of building from south showing office towers
4 North elevation showing administration building
5 Cross section

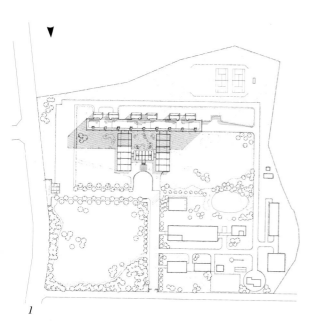

1

2

196

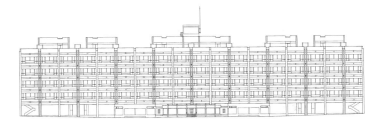

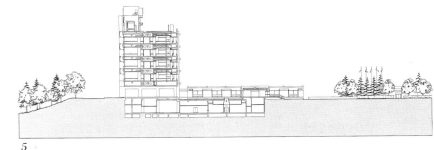

4

5

3

197

6 Interior courtyard between administration and
  laboratory building
7 Reception lobby
8 Ground-floor plan
9 Typical floor plan
10 Office tower and back of single-loaded laboratory
   corridor

6

7

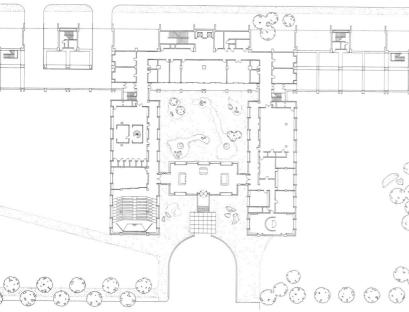

8

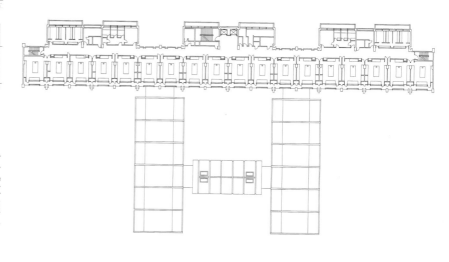

9

Teijin Applied Textile Science Center
Osaka, Japan, 1964
Client: Teijin Limited, Tokyo, Japan
with: Ohbayashi-Gumu Design Department

1 Aerial view of complex showing main facility and
  employee housing
2 Second-floor plan with courtyards
3 Cross section through employee terrace, cafeteria,
  and reception lobby
4 Cross section through employee entrances,
  courtyards, and upper level mechanical plant
5 View of employee entries and stair towers
6 View of entrance to employee cafeteria
7 Cross section of typical detail

1

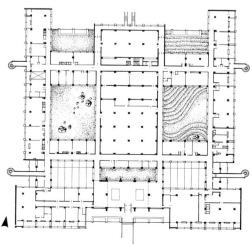

2

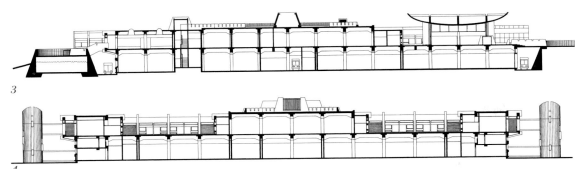

3

4

5

6

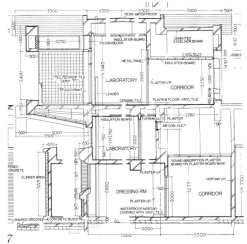

7

201

8

9

10

Donovan Pool House
Sands Point, Long Island, 1967
Client: Mr. and Mrs. Hedley Donovan
with: Joseph L. Fleischer

1 *View of exterior, facing pool*
2 *Site plan*
3 *Interior view*

1

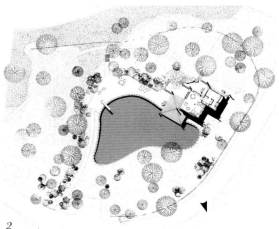

2

1

1 *Exterior view of corner employee cafeteria*
2 *View of Service Building Two from corner*
  employee cafeteria

2

3 *Perspective section showing relationship of*
  structure and services to building form
4 *Site plan*

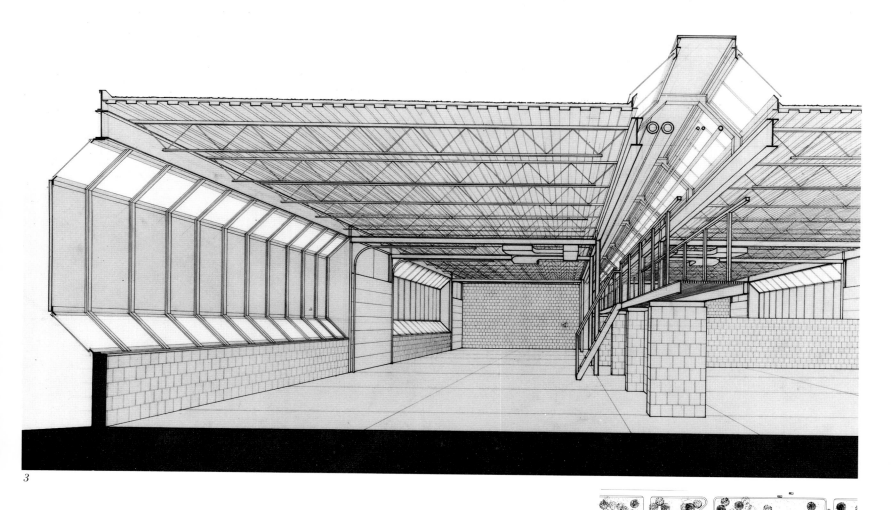

3

4

Atlantic Terminal Public Housing
Atlantic Terminal, Brooklyn, New York, 1971
Client: New York City Public Housing
Authority, New York, New York
with: Joseph L. Fleischer, Howard Kaplan,
Dimitri Linard

1 View of building showing day school at base
2 Site and typical floor plan
3 Aerial view of towers and core

1

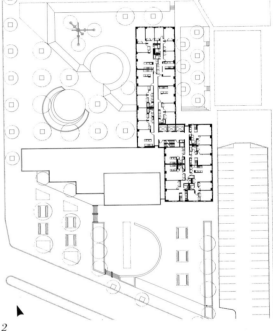

2

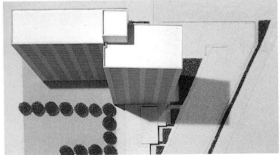

3

Englewood Public Works Facility
Englewood, New Jersey, 1973
Client: City of Englewood
with: W. Todd Springer, Joseph L. Fleischer

1

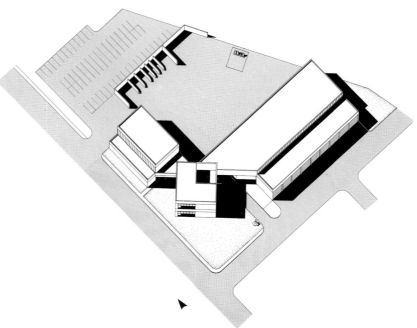

2

1 Intersection of office building and garage
2 Axonometric showing three-part organization of
  complex: offices, garages, and repair shops
3 View of intersection of office building and garages
4 Corner detail of office building

3

4

Old Westbury Campus Physical Education Building

Old Westbury, New York, 1975
Client: State University Construction Fund,
Albany, New York
with: W. Todd Springer, Joseph L. Fleischer,
Howard Sussel

1 *Main entrance, between pool and gymnasium
  structures*
2 *Aerial view*
3 *Site and floor plan*
4 *Galleria entrance*

1

2

3

4

Harlem Shopping Mall
New York, New York, 1978
Client: Corland Corporation
with: Bond Ryder James (joint venture),
Joseph L. Fleischer, W. Todd Springer,
James G. Garrison

1 *Axonometric of site*
2 *View from east of main entrance to mall*
3 *East elevation*
4 *North elevation*
5 *West elevation*

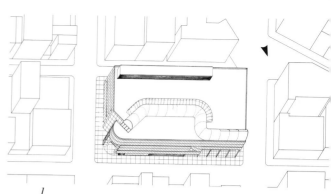

1

2

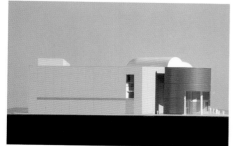

3

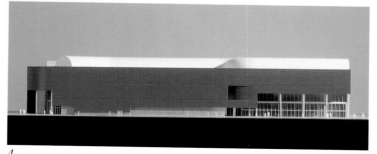

4

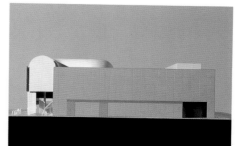

5

West Side Operations Center
New York, New York, 1978
Client: Consolidated Edison Company
with: Tyler H. Donaldson, W. Todd Springer

1 Corner showing masonry transition
2 View from street
3 Facade detail
4 Site plan

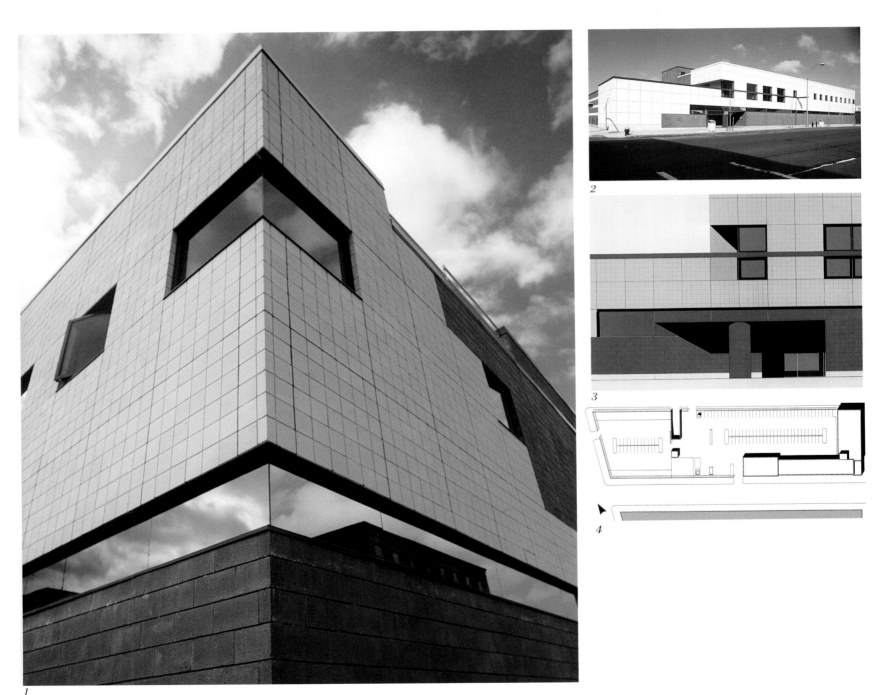

1

2

3

4

215

U.S. Embassy: Oman
Muscat, Oman, 1980–84
Client: U.S. Department of State
Scheme I with: Paul S. Byard, Duncan R.
Hazard, Todd H. Schliemann
Scheme II with: Joseph L. Fleischer, James
G. Garrison, James R. Gainfort, Sara
Elizabeth Caples, Charmian Place (interior
designer)

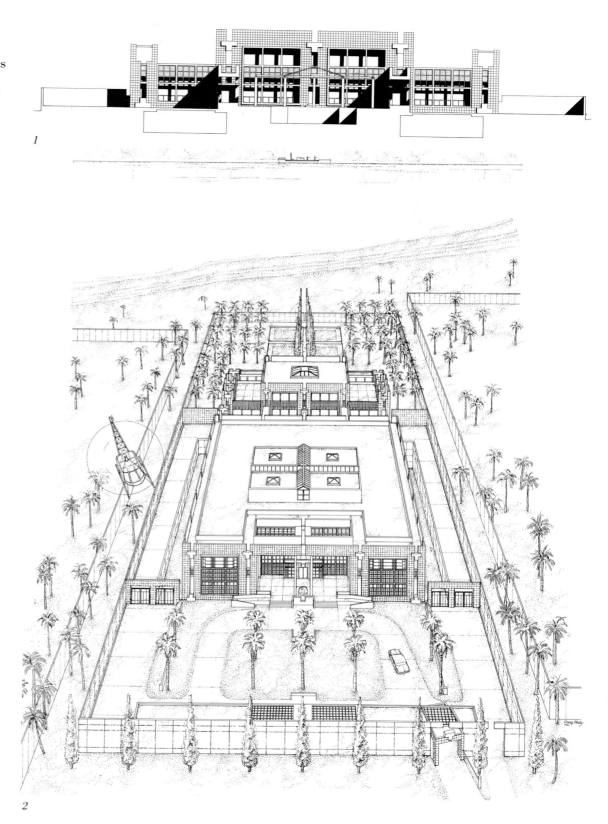

1

2

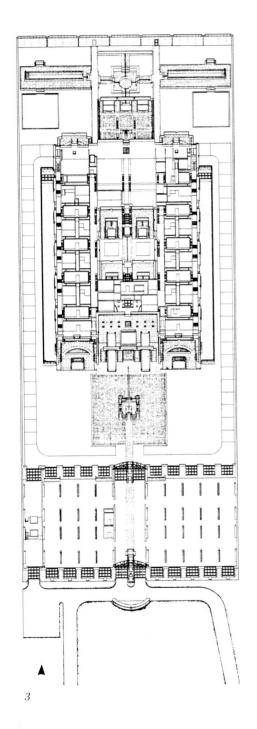

3

4

217

5 Scheme II. Two-bay model of facade
6 Scheme II. Plan and elevation detail
7 Scheme II. Cross section through enclosed
   courtyard and double exterior walls
8 Scheme II. Perspective of main entrance

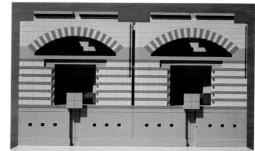

5

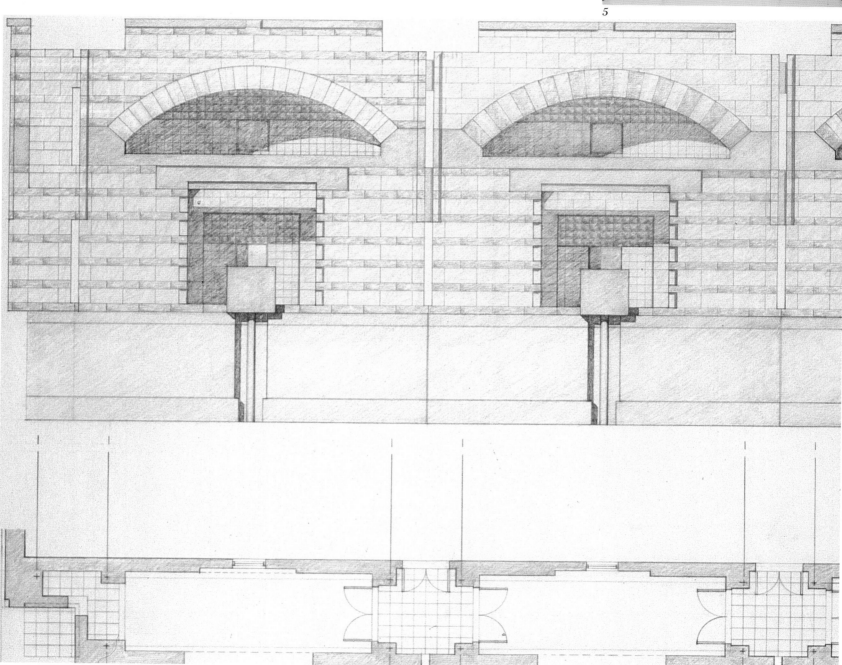

6

7

8

Peak Competition

Hong Kong, 1984

with: James G. Garrison

1,2 *Interior perspectives*
3 *Axonometric view*
4 *Site plan*

1

2

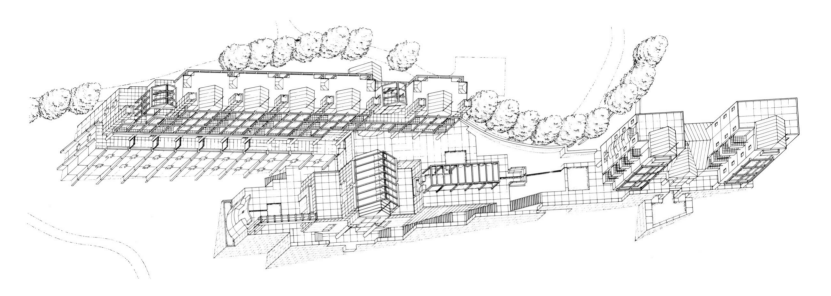

3

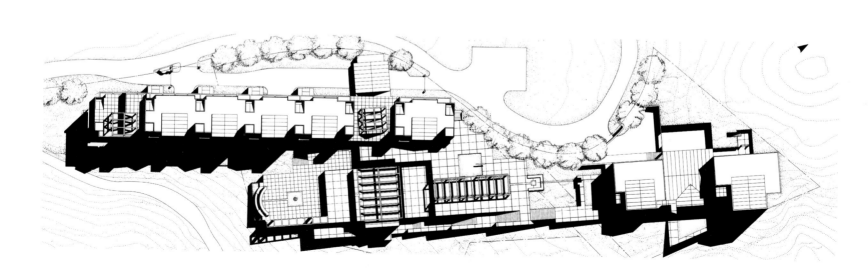

4

A Living Memorial to the Holocaust Museum of Jewish Heritage

New York, New York, 1985
Client: New York Holocaust Memorial
Commission
with: Joseph L. Fleischer, Timothy P.
Hartung, Richard Olcott, Gaston Silva, Susan
Rodriguez

1 *Site plan of Battery Park City showing museum*
2 *Entry-level plan*
3 *Below grade core exhibit plan*

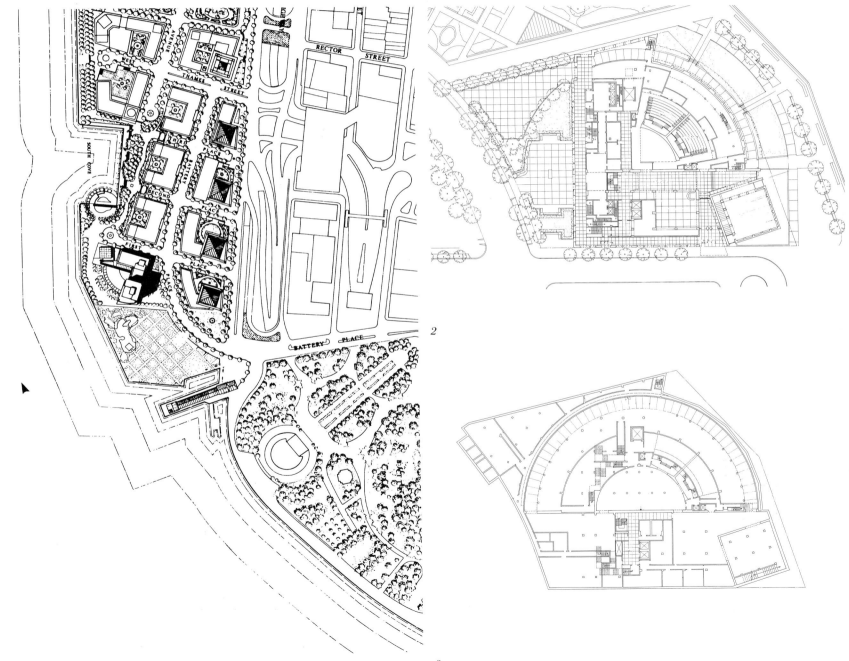

1

2

3

221

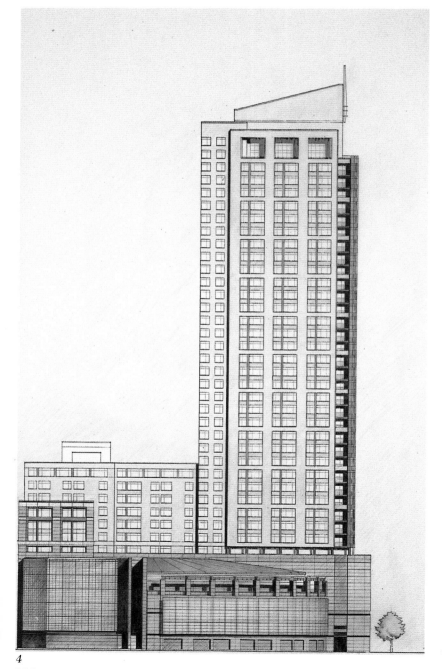

4

5

6

7

8

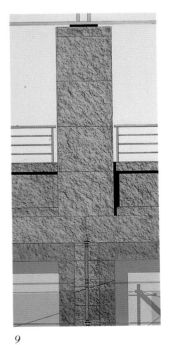

9

Hudson Valley Festival of the Arts *study*
Annandale-on-Hudson, New York, 1985
Client: Hudson Valley Festival of the Arts
with: James G. Garrison, Timothy P. Hartung

1 Perspective of shed and fly
2 Side elevation
3 Front elevation

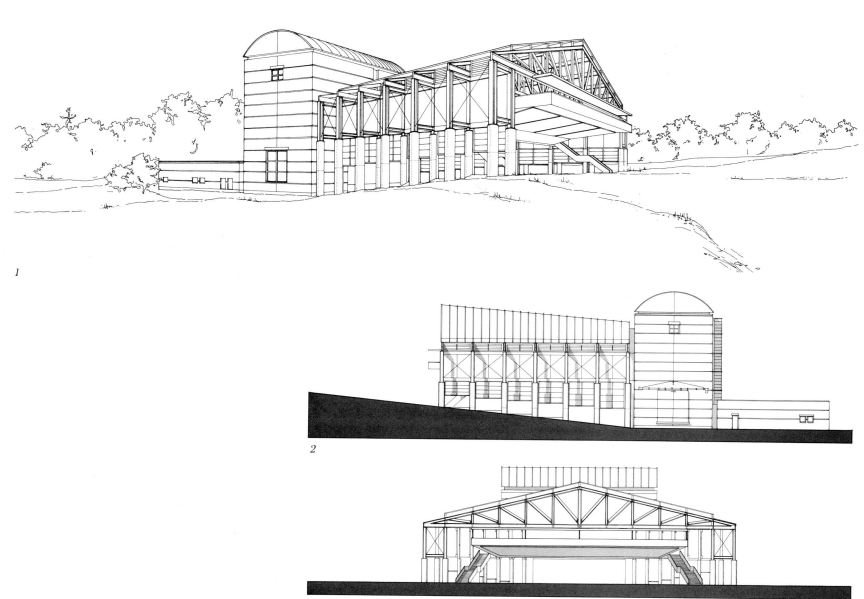

1

2

3

York College Theater
Jamaica, Queens, 1985
Client: City University of New York
with: Joseph L. Fleischer, Gaston Silva, Neil
Denari, Jihyon Kim

1 Sketch of main entrance and lobby
2 Sketch of longitudinal section through large
  theater
3 Site plan

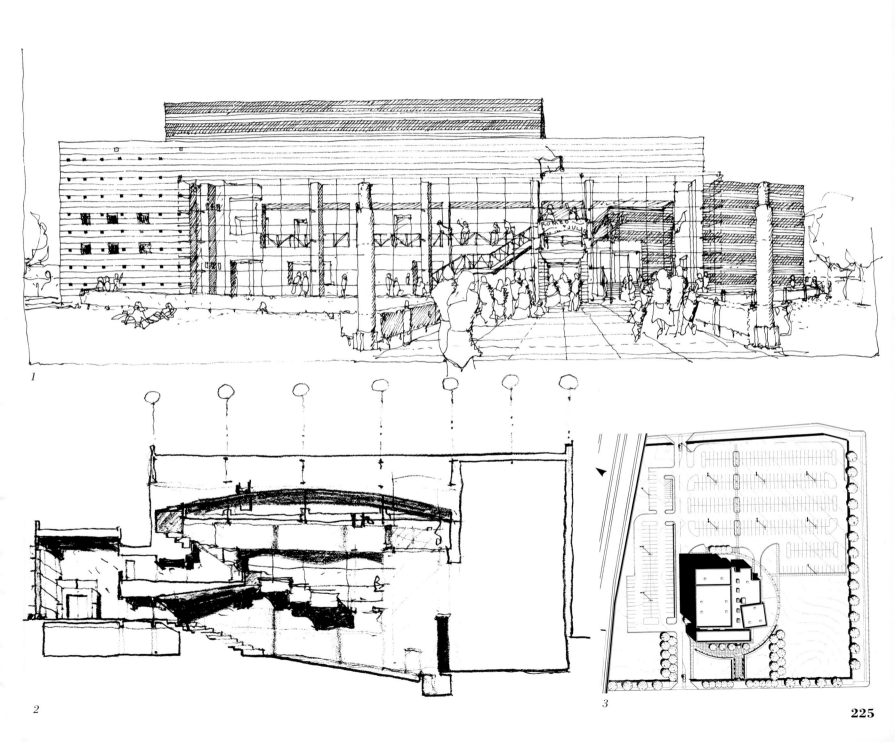

1

2

3

first is imagery—that is, what the client wishes to convey about the corporation or institution to their own staff and to their clients and the public. The second involves systems of circulation—how and where they connect to one another and to the dedicated spaces they serve, and the role they play in encouraging or discouraging social interaction. An industrial design project and an exhibition design project are also included in the section. The utilitarian design of small objects supports a belief that technology and formal expression are indivisible. Exhibition design involves the same principles of mobility that characterize any architectural project. But these projects also involve collaboration with graphic artists, writers, filmmakers, and curators. It is the communication of specific information and larger ideas that is the architectural challenge. The social value of design is no less important in interior, industrial, and exhibition design than it is in architecture and urban design—only the scale and settings are different.

1 *Windyhill, Kilmalcolm, Great Britain. Charles Rennie Mackintosh, 1901*
2 *Maison de verre, Paris, France. Pierre Chareau and Bernard Bijovoet. 1931*
3 *Sir John Soane's Museum, London, England. Sir John Soane, 1812*
4 *Brion-Vega Tomb and Cemetery, San Vito, Treviso, Italy. Carlo Scarpa, 1972*

"Rise of an American Architecture"
centennial exhibition design
New York, New York, 1969
Client: Metropolitan Museum of Art
with: Arnold Saks (graphic designer), Carl
Berger

1

1 Entrance to exhibition
2 Typical panel configuration
3 Construction diagram of typical panel

2

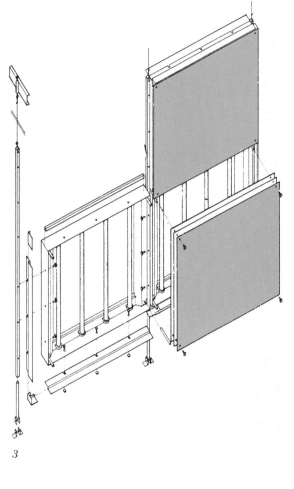

3

Offices for Simon & Schuster, Inc.
New York, New York, 1976
Client: Simon & Schuster
with: W. Todd Springer

1 View of "main street" corridor and departmental
  "alley"
2 Plan of principal floor showing circulation concept
3 Rare-book library
4 Reception area
5 Employee lounge and lending library
6 Secondary "street" and editorial offices

1

2

3

4

5

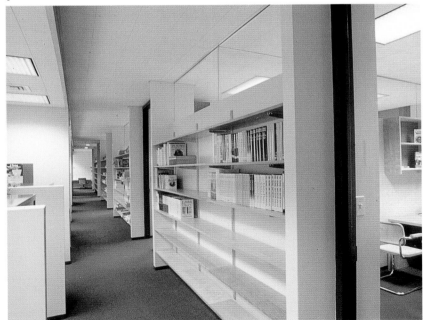

6

Consolidated Edison District 2
Business Office *interior*
East 87th Street, New York, New York, 1978
Client: Consolidated Edison Company
with: W. Todd Springer

1 *Interior view with neon logotypes*
2 *Ground-floor plan*

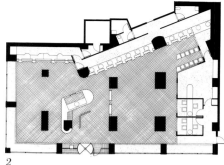

2

1

**Consolidated Edison District 6
Business Office** *renovation and interior*
West 181st Street, New York, New York,
1978
Client: Consolidated Edison Company
with: W. Todd Springer

1 Interior view of main business floor
2 Ground-floor plan

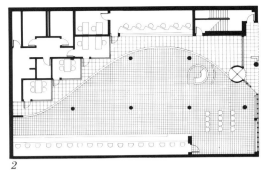

2

1

233

Offices for Norlin Corp. *interior*
White Plains, New York, 1978
Client: Norlin Corp.
with: Marla Appelbaum

1 *Primary circulation corridor with display niches*
2 *Axonometric of office plan*
3 *Entry gallery*
4 *Junior executive offices*
5 *Staff dining room*
6 *Boardroom*

1

234

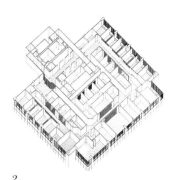

2

3

4

5

6

Offices for Backer and Spielvogel, Inc.
interior
New York, New York, 1979
Client: Backer and Spielvogel, Inc.
with: James G. Garrison, Marla Appelbaum,
Charmian Place (interior designer)

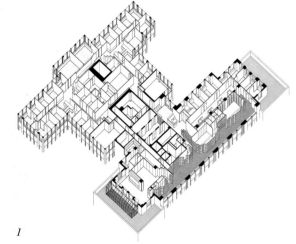

1

2

1 Axonometric of principal office floor showing
   perimeter gallery
2 Perimeter gallery showing translucent screen-wall
3 Interior corridor with asymmetrical lighting
   showing interconnecting stairway

3

4 *Gallery lounge*
5 *Waiting room and secretarial area*
6 *Main entrance*

6

5

Offices for the Securities Groups
New York, New York, 1980
Client: The Securities Groups
with: Marla Appelbaum, Dan Bernstein,
Charmian Place (interior designer)

1

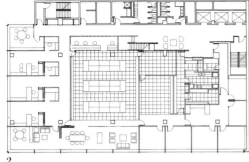

2

3

4

AMRO Bank
New York, New York, 1980
Client: Amsterdam Rotterdam Bank, New
York, New York
with: Paul S. Byard, James G. Garrison,
Marla Appelbaum, Charmian Place (interior
designer)

1 Second-floor reception area showing black glass
   balustrade and translucent glass screen-wall
2 Second-floor plan
3 Corridor between interior office open area and
   exterior private office area
4 Banking floor
5 Stairway and glass screen detail

1

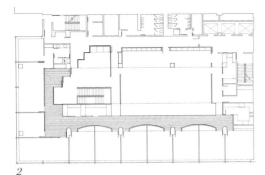

2

3

4

5

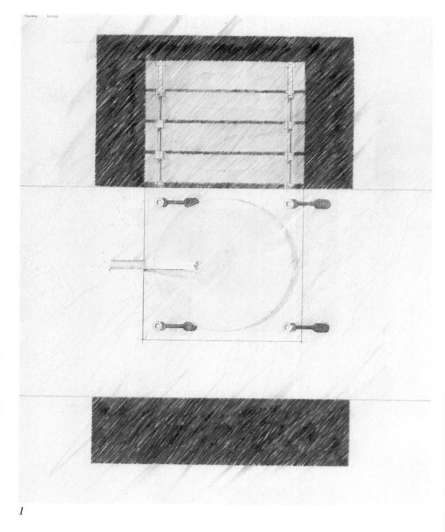

1

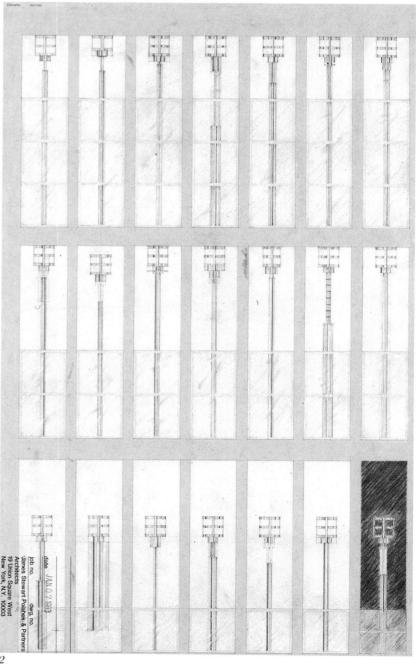

2

1 *Design for stacking ashtrays*
2 *Alternative designs for crystal and silver*
   candelabrum
3 *Candle holder*
4 *Prototype for condiment set*

3

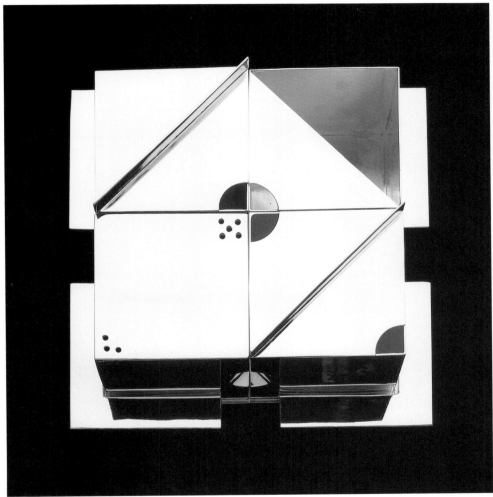

4

**Offices for James Stewart Polshek
and Partners**
New York, New York, 1985
with: Joseph L. Fleischer, James G.
Garrison, Timothy P. Hartung, Todd H.
Schliemann, Tyler H. Donaldson, Richard M.
Olcott

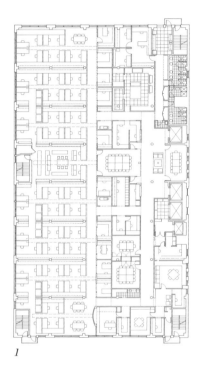

1

2

1 Floor plan
2 Main reception area
3 Interior detail

3

Commissions

Asterisk indicates work illustrated in this book.

1957

Residence I for Dr. and Mrs. Gerald Oster*
Stony Point, New York
(with Ludovica Schniewind)

1960

Residence II for Dr. and Mrs. Gerald Oster*
New York, New York
interior

1963

Teijin Central Research Institute*
Tokyo, Japan

1964

Teijin Applied Textile Science Center*
Osaka, Japan

Residence for Mr. and Mrs. Ronald Stanton
New York, New York
interior

Residence for Mr. and Mrs. Joseph Miller
New York, New York
interior

Residence for Ms. Anna Neisser
New York, New York
interior

1965

Loft's Pond Park Pavilion*
Baldwin, Long Island

Residence for Mr. and Mrs. Lloyd Richards
New York, New York
interior

Offices for Shulman-Sunshine
New York, New York
interior

George Kovacs Store
New York, New York
interior

Residence for John Cates, M.D.
New York, New York
interior

Children's Psychiatric Hospital
West Seneca, New York
design consultation

1966

Residence for Ambassador and Mrs. Franklin Williams
New York, New York
interior

55 West 42 Street Lobby
New York, New York
interior

Reston Commercial Center
Reston, Virginia
project

Residence for Mr. and Mrs. Hugo Dunhill
New York, New York
interior

Residential Treatment Center for Big Brothers, Inc.*
New York, New York
(with Walfredo Toscanini)
renovation and interior; demolished

1967

Stable Quadrangle Academic Center
State University College at Old Westbury
Old Westbury, New York
project

Residence for Mr. and Mrs. Eric Lomnitz
New York, New York
demolished

Bedford-Stuyvesant Community Center*
Brooklyn, New York
project

U.S. Pavilion for Expo '70*
Osaka, Japan
(with Arnold Saks)
invited competition

Pool House for Mr. and Mrs. Hedley Donovan*
Sands Point, Long Island

Offices for International Ore and Fertilizer Corporation
New York, New York
interior

Residence for Mr. and Mrs. Peter Ryan
Newtown, Connecticut
project

1968

New York State Bar Center*
Albany, New York
restoration, addition, and interior

Atlantic Terminal Urban Renewal Area Concept Plan*
Housing Development Authority
Brooklyn, New York
study

Psychology Department Offices
Brooklyn College
Brooklyn, New York
interior

Residence for Mr. and Mrs. Monte Ghertler
New York, New York
interior

Residence for Mr. and Mrs. Edgar Bronfman
New York, New York
interior

Residence for Mr. and Mrs. Milton Carrow
New York, New York
interior

Residence for Mr. and Mrs. Binem Krygier
New York, New York
interior

Offices for Athlone Industries
New York, New York
interior

Offices for Transammonia
New York, New York
interior

Office and Library for Mr. Mark Millard
New York, New York
interior

Clinton Youth and Family Center*
New York, New York
(with Walfredo Toscanini)
renovation and interior; demolished

Old Westbury Campus Service Group*
State University College at Old Westbury
Old Westbury, New York

Tea Lane Property
Chilmark, Massachusetts
project

1969

Recreation Pavilion for Mr. and Mrs. Edgar Bronfman*
Purchase, New York

Roscher Gripcomat for Mr. Martin Shulman
exhibition display; demolished

Choate-Rosemary Hall Campus*
Rosemary Hall/The Choate School
Wallingford, Connecticut

Allied Chemical Materials Research Center*
Allied Chemical Corporation
Morristown, New Jersey
renovation and addition

Quinco Mental Health Center*
Region 10 Foundation
Columbus, Indiana

Residence for Mr. and Mrs. Robert Gellert
Chappaqua, New York

Twin Parks East Housing*
New York State Urban Development Corporation
New York, New York

Georg Jensen Store*
New York, New York
demolished

"Rise of An American Architecture"*
Metropolitan Museum of Art Centennial Exhibition
New York, New York

Kingsborough Community College Health and Physical Education Building*
Kingsborough Community College
City University of New York
Brooklyn, New York

Master Plan for Jewish Museum
New York, New York
study

Wesleyan University Student Center and Central Plant*
Wesleyan University
Middletown, Connecticut
project

1970

Undergraduate Dormitory
Wesleyan University
Middletown, Connecticut
study

Educational Testing Service Conference Center
Princeton, New Jersey
project

1971

Atlantic Terminal Public Housing*
New York City Public Housing Authority
Atlantic Terminal Urban Renewal Area
Brooklyn, New York

Bus Shelter
Department of Highways
New York, New York

Residence for Mr. and Mrs. Hedley Donovan
New York, New York
interior

Offices for Weber Insurance Co.
New York, New York
interior

Paterson New Jersey Master Plan*
Paterson Redevelopment Authority
Paterson, New Jersey
study

Science Building
Choate School
Wallingford, Connecticut
project

1972

Showroom for Sonneman Inc.
New York, New York
demolished

Vassar College Student Housing
Purchase, New York
project

Crossroads School
New York, New York
study

Recycle Fuels Plant
Westinghouse Electric Corporation
Columbia, South Carolina
project

Residence for Dr. and Mrs. Zimmerman
Rumson, New Jersey
renovation and interior design

1973

Intermediate School 172*
New York, New York
project

Englewood Public Works Facility*
Englewood, New Jersey

Westinghouse Prototype Turbine Plant*
Westinghouse Electric Corporation
study

Public School 165
New York, New York
project

Residence for Ms. Ruth Franklin
Greenwich, Connecticut

Helen Owens Carey Playhouse and Chelsea Theater
Brooklyn Academy of Music
Brooklyn, New York
renovation

1974

Brotherhood Synagogue*
New York, New York
restoration

Rubella Laboratory
Department of Pediatrics
Roosevelt Hospital
New York, New York
interior

1975

Old Westbury Campus Physical Education Building*
State University College at Old Westbury
Old Westbury, New York

New Mexico Rehabilitation Center
Roswell, New Mexico
study

1976

Empire State Plaza
Albany, New York
study

Allied Chemical Corporation Master Plan
Morristown, New Jersey
study

Offices for Simon & Schuster, Inc.*
New York, New York
interior

Day School
Church of the Heavenly Rest
New York, New York
interior

1977

Offices for Lombard-Wall
New York, New York
interior; demolished

Sajale Jewelry Showroom
New York, New York
project

State Office Building
Delhi, New York
study

Ocean State Theater
Providence, Rhode Island
study

Skidmore College Housing
Saratoga Springs, New York
competition

Hillburn Recreation Center
Hillburn, New York
project

Roosevelt Island
Roosevelt Island Development Corporation
New York, New York
design consultation

Trancas Medical Center*
Trancas Associates
Napa, California
(with Peter Gluck and Associates)

The Urban Center and Bookstore*
New York, New York
restoration and interior design

Southhold Estate
Long Island, New York
study

Brotherhood Synagogue Memorial Garden*
New York, New York

Residence for Mr. and Mrs. Michael Korda
New York, New York
interior

Offices and Studio for Landeck Productions, Inc.
New York, New York
project

1978

Behavioral Research Lab
Roosevelt Hospital
New York, New York
project

Offices for Norlin Corp.*
White Plains, New York
interior

Residence for Mr. and Mrs. Richard E. Snyder
St. Moritz Hotel
New York, New York
interior

New York Society Library*
New York, New York
renovation and interior

U.S. Customs House*
Bowling Green, New York
(with Marcel Breuer Associates)
competition

Consolidated Edison District 2 Business Office*
New York, New York
interior

Consolidated Edison District 6 Business Office*
New York, New York
renovation and interior

West Side Operations Center*
Consolidated Edison Company
New York, New York

Harlem Shopping Mall*
Corland Corporation
New York, New York
(with Bond Ryder James)

Third World Trade Center*
Harlem Urban Development Corporation
New York, New York
study

U.S. Consulate and Residence*
Lyons, France
project

Carnegie Hall Master Plan*
New York, New York
study

1979

Energy Control Center
Consolidated Edison Company
New York, New York
interior

Hall of Fame*
Bronx Community College
Bronx, New York
restoration

Offices for Backer & Spielvogel, Inc.*
New York, New York
interior

Delafield Estates*
Delafield Estates, Ltd.
Riverdale, New York

Glenfield Middle School*
Montclair, New Jersey
renovation and addition

Jacob K. Javits Convention Center
New York, New York
programming and design consultation

1980

500 Park Avenue
New York, New York
renovation

500 Park Tower*
Equitable Life Assurance Co.
Tishman Speyer Properties
New York, New York

Offices for the Securities Groups*
New York, New York
demolished

Celine Store
New York, New York
interior

Rochester Cultural District Planning Study
Rochester Downtown Development Corporation
Rochester, New York

Union Square Mixed Use Development
Rapid America Corporation
New York, New York
project

Residence for Mr. and Mrs. Charles Atkins
New York, New York
demolished

AMRO Bank*
Amsterdam-Rotterdam Bank
New York, New York
interior

U.S. Embassy: Oman I*
Muscat, Oman
project

Association of the Bar of the City of New York*
New York, New York
renovation and interior

Offices for the Department of Parks
The Arsenal
New York, New York
project

Offices for Dillon Read & Co., Inc.
New York, New York
interior

Rochester Riverside Convention Center*
Rochester, New York

Church of the Heavenly Rest II
New York, New York
study

Rembrandt Site Study and Guidelines
Carnegie Hall
New York, New York

Residence for Mr. and Mrs. Ivan Chermayeff
New York, New York
interior

1981

Residence for Mr. and Mrs. Harry Macklowe
New York, New York
interior

Prototype Medical Suites, Metropolitan Hospital
New York, New York
renovation and interior

Offices for J. Rothschild Management Corporation
New York, New York
interior

Weill Recital Hall Lobby*
Carnegie Hall
New York, New York
renovation

Student Residence
Columbia University
New York, New York
project

1982

Second Church of Christ Scientist
New York, New York
competition

Danbury Urban Design Study
Danbury, Connecticut
study

Ferris Booth Hall Student Center
Columbia University
New York, New York
interior

Liberty House*
Mariners Cove Associates
Battery Park City
New York, New York

North County Resource Recovery Facility*
San Marcos, California

1983

44 Wall Street Lobby
New York, New York
renovation

Restoration of the Stuyvesant Fish House
New York, New York
project

Paris Opera Competition*
Paris, France

Residence for Mr. and Mrs. Larry Silverstein
New York, New York
interior

Stroh River Place Master Plan*
Detroit, Michigan

Harborside Financial Center*
Jersey City, New Jersey
renovation

Offices for Stroh Properties, Inc.
River Place
Detroit, Michigan
renovation and interior

River Place Parking Garage
Detroit, Michigan
(with Sims-Varner and Associates)

Office Building
Lincoln Properties
Atlanta, Georgia
project

Theater of Performing Arts
City of Miami Beach
Miami Beach, Florida
project

IBM Headquarters Facility*
White Plains, New York
renovation and addition

1984

Seaport West
New York, New York
project

Washington Court*
Philips International Holding Corp.
New York, New York

Dromenon Theater
New York, New York
project

Kaplan Space*
Carnegie Hall
New York, New York
interior

Peak Competition
Hong Kong, China

West Palm Beach Condominiums and Club
West Palm Beach, Florida
project

Emigrant Savings Bank*
New York, New York
renovation

Swid Powell Designs*
New York, New York

Monty's Market
South Miami, Florida
project

Carnegie Hall*
New York, New York
restoration, renovation, and interior design

Weill Recital Hall*
Carnegie Hall
New York, New York
renovation and interior design

1985

Offices for James Stewart Polshek and Partners*
New York, New York

U.S. Embassy: Oman II*
Muscat, Oman

Chene Park Housing
River Place
Detroit, Michigan
study

Drawing Center
New York, New York
interior

Grace Church School Master Plan*
New York, New York
renovation and study

Bronxville West*
Bronxville, New York

New York Coliseum Competition*
New York, New York

Eighth Avenue Residential Condominium*
Philips International Holding Corp.
New York, New York

Boston Symphony Hall Master Plan*
Boston, Massachusetts

Stroh Brewery Pub
River Place
Detroit, Michigan
project

A Living Memorial to the Holocaust Museum of Jewish Heritage*
New York Holocaust Memorial Commission
New York, New York

Residence for Mr. Frederick Field
New York, New York
project

Biscaya Hotel
Centennial Partnership, Ltd.
Miami Beach, Florida
project

Hudson Valley Festival of the Arts*
Annandale-on-Hudson, New York
study

York College Theater*
City University of New York
Jamaica, Queens, New York

Bard College Student Residence*
Annandale-on-Hudson, New York

Barnard College Student Residence*
New York, New York

Metropolitan Park Tower*
Park Tower Realty
New York, New York

Sage Hall*
Smith College
Northampton, Massachusetts
renovation

Brooklyn Museum Master Plan*
Brooklyn, New York
competition

1986

Union Theological Seminary*
General Atlantic Corporation
New York, New York
competition

Tanglewood Music Shed*
Boston Symphony Orchestra
Lenox, Massachusetts
study

Yerba Buena Theater for Performing Arts
San Francisco Redevelopment Authority
San Francisco, California

Princeton Nurseries*
Laramie-Dawson Corp.
Plainsborough and South Brunswick, New Jersey
project

Schenectady Downtown Plan
City of Schenectady
Schenectady, New York

Residential Development
Clover Farm Properties
Sherman, Connecticut

German Democratic Republic U.N. Mission
New York, New York
study

Residential Condominium
The Related Companies, Inc.
Kreisler Borg Florman
Battery Park City-Site 11
New York, New York

Boston Symphony Hall
Boston, Massachusetts
renovation

Industrial Park and Conference Center
Rochester Institute of Technology
The Farash Corporation
Rochester, New York
study

Residential Development
521–525 Park Avenue
Park Tower Realty
New York, New York
renovation and addition

Atlantixenter Urban Design Study
Philadelphia, Pennsylvania
study

Jerome Levy Economics Institute
Bard College
Annandale-on-Hudson, New York
renovation and restoration

Offices for Screen Actors Guild
New York, New York
interior

Offices for Muir Cornelius Moore
New York, New York
interior

Mid-Hudson General Mail Facility
U.S. Postal Service
Newburgh, New York

Temple Sholom
Greenwich, Connecticut
study

Broadway Center
Kossow Corporation
Schenectady, New York

1987

777 Madison Avenue
New York, New York
addition

New Jersey Cultural Center
State of New Jersey
study

Mott Street Office Building
Mott Street Joint Venture
New York, New York

Snug Harbor Music Hall Theater
Staten Island, New York
competition

East 88 Street Residential Development
General Atlantic Corporation
New York, New York

Kingsport Civic Center
City of Kingsport
Kingsport, Tennessee

George Washington Hall
Phillips Andover Academy
Andover, Massachusetts
addition and renovation

Hall Auditorium
Oberlin College
Oberlin, Ohio
addition and renovation

1988

Brooklyn College Master Plan and Ingersoll Hall
Brooklyn, New York
study and renovation

IBM Enterprise Systems Group
Sterling Forest, New York
renovation

Siegel Cooper Department Store
Tishman Speyer Properties
New York, New York
addition and renovation

Selected Bibliography

1959

Kellogg, Cynthia. "Space with Separation." *New York Times*, August 2: 30.

1963

"Project for Research Center for Teikoku Jinken Co." *Japan Architect*, April: 26–28.

1964

"Functional Grid in Japan." *Architectural Forum*, August–September: 131–35.

Nichols, Kenneth. "Leaves Mark on Japan." *Akron Beacon Journal*, December 2: F2.

1965

"An American Castle in Japan." *Fortune*, May.

1966

"A New York, Studio di Architettura al Quarantasettesimo Piano." *Domus*, February: 17–19.

"Innovation: Town House." *House Beautiful*, July: 61–64.

"An Overlooked Bargain: Bright Young Men with Designs on the Future." *Fortune*, July: 123.

"Fluid Space." *Progressive Architecture*, September: 138–39.

1968

"An Old Station House Gets A New Mission." *Architectural Forum*, March: 50–53.

Huxtable, Ada Louise. "This Time Everyone Wins." *New York Times*, July 21.

"The U.S. at Osaka: Assemblage of Pods." *Architectural Forum*, October: 59.

1969

Grant, Susan. "The West Side." *Home Furnishings Daily*, May 23.

1970

"Teahouse by the Pool." *Architectural Forum*, May: 52–53.

Huxtable, Ada Louise. "The Tower, the House, and the Park." *New York Times*, May 17.

"Magazine Reviews Plans for Mental Health Center." *The Republic*, Columbus, Indiana, June 5.

McQuade, Walter. "Beauties Left Over from a Fat-Cigar World." *Life*, August 14: 29.

"New Image for Jensen's." *Progressive Architecture*, September: 32.

Huxtable, Ada Louise. *Will They Ever Finish Bruckner Boulevard?* New York, Macmillan Publications.

1971

Huxtable, Ada Louise. "Not for the Medici." *New York Times*, January 31.

Morgan, James D. "Design for Merchandising." *Architectural Record*, February: 89.

Jensen, Robert. "Clinton Youth and Family Center." *Architectural Record*, June: 107–110.

Huxtable, Ada Louise. "New Bar Center Offers Lesson in Civilized Architecture." *New York Times*, September 25.

"A New Building in Albany Dramatically Unites Tradition and Creativity." *Architectural Record*, December: 94.

1972

"Utilitarian Flexibility for Old Westbury College." *Architectural Record*, February: 47–49.

Kennedy, William. "Work in Progress/James Polshek." *Intellectual Digest*, February: 8.

Seymour, Whitney North, Jr. "Smart, These Lawyers." *American Bar Association Journal*, March: 31–33.

Collins, Libby. "New Horizons." *The Greenwich Social Review*, March: 16–25.

"New York State Bar Center." *AIA Journal*, May: 33.

Baird, Weldon. "Quinco Center: A 5-County Effort." *The Republic*, Columbus, Indiana, September 29.

1973

Morgan, Jim. "A Bridge to Health." *Architecture Plus*, June: 30–32.

"Rosemary and Time." *Architectural Forum*, September: 48–55.

1974

"Twin Parks East." *A + U*, June.

"Carefully Phased Construction Produced Substantial Savings on Allied Chemicals New Research Center." *Architectural Record*, August: 127–30.

1975

"Rosemary Hall—Schule, Wallingfort, U.S.A." *Baumeister* 3, March: 617.

"Neurologische Klinik in Columbus, U.S.A." *Baumeister* 6, June: 509.

Huxtable, Ada Louise. "Recycling A Landmark for Today." *New York Times*, June 15.

1976

Gill, Brendan. "BAM Grows in Brooklyn." *New York Times Magazine*, October 24: 20–21.

1977

Filler, Martin. "One for the Books." *Progressive Architecture*, September: 20.

Goldberger, Paul. "Good Lessons in Creating Working Quarters That Work." *New York Times*, October 20: III, 10.

1978

"The Industrial Esthetic: Two Buildings by James Stewart Polshek and Partners." *Architectural Record*, February: 107–109.

"James Stewart Polshek and Partners." *Space Design*, July: 3–56.

Lessard, Suzannah. "The Towers of Light." *New Yorker*, July 10: 32–58.

1980

Emanuel, Muriel, ed. *Contemporary Architects*. New York: St. Martin's Press, 632–34.

Diamonstein, Barbaralee. *American Architecture Now*. New York: Rizzoli International Publications, 183–205.

"Design Awards Program—Award, A New Headquarters for the New York State Bar Association." *Progressive Architecture*, January: 136.

"Projet d'un consulat, Lyon." *L'Architecture d'Aujourd-'hui*, February: 61–64.

Huxtable, Ada Louise. "An Enlightened Plan for Converting the Customs House." *New York Times*, June 1: II, 25.

1981

"Architectural Design Citation, U.S. Consular Residence and Office, Lyons, France." *Progressive Architecture*, January: 130–31.

"Architectural Design Citation, Glenfield Middle School, Montclair, New Jersey." *Progressive Architecture*, January: 132.

Goldberger, Paul. "31 Prizes Are Given for Distinguished Architecture." *New York Times*, January 17: 14.

"Healthcare in Napa, California: Accommodation and Integration." *Architectural Record*, April: 112–17.

Huxtable, Ada Louise. "500 Park—A Skillful Solution." *New York Times*, May 3: II, 27.

Myers, Jim. "Rochester Redesign." *Sunday Democrat and Chronicle*, Rochester, New York May 31.

Doubilet, Susan. "The Classical Transformed." *Progressive Architecture*, October: 105.

Wiseman, Carter. "Power to the People." *New York*, October 5.

Morton, David. "The Best of Both Worlds?" *Progressive Architecture*, November: 96–101.

"James Polshek." *Sunday Democrat and Chronicle*, Rochester, New York, November 15.

1982

"Offices for Backer & Spielvogel, Inc." *Architectural Record*, mid February: 114–16.

Goldberger, Paul. "A Superb Scheme for the Renovation of Carnegie Hall." *New York Times*, March 7: II, 27.

"Repairs Renew Historic Colonnade." *Engineering News Record* 209, no. 15, October 7: 58–59.

1983

Kennedy, William. *O Albany!* New York: The Viking Press.

"Architectural Design Citation, Rochester Convention Center, Rochester, NY." *Progressive Architecture*, January: 92.

"Con Edison Builds a More Livable New York." *Corporate Design*, January–February: 42–51.

Amery, Colin. "London Observer Views New York." *Skyline*, April: 11–13.

Goldberger, Paul. "Carnegie Hall Restoration, Phase 1." *New York Times*, September 8: III, 16.

Wiseman, Carter. "Setting New Standards for Sensitive Innovation on Park Avenue." *New York*, September 19: 59.

1984

"500 Park Tower." *Baumeister* 2, February: 40.

"J.S. Polshek." *Space Design*, June: 36.

Wiseman, Carter. "Good Neighbor Policy." *Architectural Record*, July: 95–97.

"Findlay, Steven. "Stroh's Uncaps Historic River Place." *Daily Tribune*, Royal Oak, Michigan, July 14.

Benson, Robert. "River Place—Stroh's Dream for Detroit." *Detroit News*, July 24.

Kissel, Howard. "A Modernist Builds for the Future." *Women's Wear Daily*, July 31.

Goldberger, Paul. "Defining Luxury in New York's New Apartments." *New York Times*, August 16: III, 1.

Severo, Richard. "Battle Over Cornices and Lintels Rages in 'Village'." *New York Times*, August 28: II, 1.

Marpillero, Sandro. "International Architecture Review, Renascence and Illusion: Battery Park City and Other Stories." *Casabella*, November: 16.

"Stroh Brewery Company." *Corporate Design & Realty*, November/December: 15.

Miro, Marsha. "Riverfront Past, Present, and Future Are Partners in Revival Area." *Detroit Free Press*, November 29: C1.

1985

"Architectural Design Citation, Delafield Estate." *Progressive Architecture*, January: 122–23.

Wiseman, Carter. "High Rise, Hard Sell." *New York*, March 11: 42–46.

Holusha, John. "Detroit Embarks on the Greening of its Riverfront." *New York Times*, April 29: I, 12.

Freedman, Samuel G. "The Glory of Carnegie Hall." *New York Times Magazine*, May 19: VI, 44.

Zeeman, Diane. "Leading Firm to Design West Side Project." *Review-Press Reporter*, Bronxville, New York, September 26.

Truppin, Andrea. "Public Space Experience." *Interiors*, November: cover, 111–21.

Sokolov, Raymond. "Retreading Motown: New Oases in the Urban Desert." *Wall Street Journal*, November 5: 28.

Miro, Marsha. "Stroh's Project Won't Ignore Past." *Detroit Free Press*, November 15: B1.

Latour, Alessandra and Thomas Stetz. "Glenfield Middle School." *L'Industria delle Construzioni*, December: 48–53.

"James Stewart Polshek." *Process: Architecture* 64.

1986

"Forum USA." *Werk, Bauen + Wohnen*, January/February: 18–19.

Russell, Beverly. "Verdict from the Jury." *Interiors*, January: 156.

Posner, Ellen. "Architecture: Computers Do It Faster." *Wall Street Journal*, February 25: 28.

"Preserving Democracy." *Professional Office Design*, summer.

McCain, Mark. "Can Savvy Architect Sell Tower on Park?" *Crain's New York Business*, June 2: 3.

Wiseman, Carter. "The Next Great Place." *New York*, June 16: 34–38.

Robinson, Cervin. "Contextual Tower Rises Above a 50's Classic." *Architecture*, July: 86–89.

"Restoration." *New Yorker*, July 7: 20–22.

Korman, Richard. "Orchestrating a Carnegie Overhaul." *Engineering News-Record*, August 21: 15.

Tom, Dominic. "Fla. Builder Plans $80 M. Office Project Near Canal Square." *Schenectady Gazette*, August 27.

"James Stewart Polshek." *Toshi-Jutaku*, September: 17–20.

Berger, Joseph. "Holocaust Memorial to Rise Near Battery Park." *New York Times*, September 5: 1.

Giovannini, Joseph. "Museum's Design Is Based on Promising Concept." *New York Times*, September 5: B4.

Kimball, Roger. "A Village Vanguard." *Architectural Record*, October: 90–95.

Koch, Liz. "Unveil Winning Design for Brooklyn's Museum." *The Phoenix*, October 16: 1.

Giovannini, Joseph. "Brooklyn Museum Design Selected." *New York Times*, October 17: III, 40.

Hine, Thomas. "An Attention-Getting Design for the Brooklyn Museum." *Philadelphia Enquirer*, October 26.

Heck, L.S. "Isozaki/Polshek Team Selected for Brooklyn Museum Addition." *Architecture*, December: 19.

Roberts, Rex. "Columbia Plays Carnegie Hall." *Columbia, Magazine of Columbia University*, December: 16–24.

Goldberger, Paul. "Carnegie's Allegro Facelift: Past Lives." *New York Times*, December 2: II, 1.

Knight, Carleton III. "Carnegie Hall." *Christian Science Monitor*, December 26: 14–15.

1987

Ryder, Sharon Lee. "Carnegie Hall: Better Than Ever." *Architecture*, February: 76–80.

Doubilet, Susan. "Mixed Metaphors." *Progressive Architecture*, February: 80–85.

Rottenbach, Jane. "A Great Hall is Made Even Greater." *Lighting Design & Application*, February: 4–7.

Porter, Andrew. "Musical Events, Chamber." *New Yorker*, February 23: 101–104.

Davis, Douglas. "Winging It: Does Adding On Add Up?" *Newsweek*, February 23: 70–73.

Goldberger, Paul. "Good Design, Bad Site—Poor Timing." *New York Times*, March 29: II, 34.

Arky, Beth. "Battle Lines Drawn on Club Building Plan." *Crain's New York Business*, March 30: 27.

James Stewart Polshek and Partners (1980–)

Partners

Joseph L. Fleischer	Partner 1980– Associate 1970–1979
Timothy P. Hartung	Partner 1987– Associate 1980–1986
James G. Garrison	Partner 1987– Associate 1981–1986
Paul S. Byard	Partner 1980–1986

Associates

Marla Appelbaum	Senior Associate 1987– Associate 1980–1986
Tyler H. Donaldson	Senior Associate 1987– Associate 1981–1986
Duncan R. Hazard	Senior Associate 1987– Associate 1983–1986
Sara Elizabeth Caples	1984–
Richard M. Olcott	1985–
Todd H. Schliemann	1985–
Gaston Silva	1987–
James R. Gainfort	1984–1986
Cyntha D. Thompson	1984–1985

James Stewart Polshek and Associates (1970–1979)

Associates

Howard M. Kaplan	1970–1972
Dimitri Linard	1970–1976
W. Todd Springer	1970–1979
Sean W. Sculley	1973–1975

Staff (1964–)

Richard Alden
Molly Alpert
Jon Ambrose
John Amisano
Eduardo Andeade
John Anderson
Charles Ayes
Margaret Azzoni
Pamela Babey
Manuel Baez
David Barabas
Richard Basta
Arlene Batwin
Beth Beranbaum
Ray Beeler
Michael Benzemann
William Berg
Carl Berger
Deborah Berkson
Dan Bernstein
Ditia Blinn
David Bliss
Lucia Bogotay
Christine Bolender
William Boling
Carlos Bondoc
Anne Boxall
Leesa Bradley
Van Brody
David Bylund
David Cagle
Charles Calcagni
Craig Cameron
James Carlin
Kurt Carlson
Howei Chan
Joan Chan
Steve Cinco
Travis Cloud
Mike Connell
Steve Corelli
Doug Cutsogeorge
Glen DaCosta
Susan Davis-McCarter
Margaret DeBolt
Olvia Demetriou
Mary Dempsey
Neil Denari
William Derman
Uday Dhar
Deborah Dietsch
Donald Dixon
Greg Doench
Fred Drohsler
Jane Duff
Mario Egozi
Amy Eliot
Harold Ellis
Susanna Epelbaum
Christopher Eseman
Donald Evans
Elaine Felhandler
William Fellows
Mark Fisher

Tony Fowler
Philip Furness
Leonard Fusco
Walter Ganley
William Garbus
John Garment
Daniel Gladstone
Wendy Glomb
Pat Golden
Ellen Goldstein
Michael Golubov
George Gonzalez
Terrance Goode
T. J. Gottesdiener
Michael Grabman
Sharon Grau
Susan Green
William Griffin
Margaret Griffin
Charles Griffith
Eva Growney
Thaddeus Hanser
Mojgan Hariri
Michael Harrington
Lee Harris
Sara Hart
Emily Harvey
John Harvey
Jay Haverson
Michael Herlands
Nancy Hertzfeld
Arthur Jay Hibbs
Stephen Hicks
Angeline Ho
James Hoffman
Alison Holt
Herman Howard
Margaret Howard
Lisa Huberman
William Hyman
Kristof Jacunski
Peter Jensen
Rangini Kalappa
John Kaliski
Ann Kalla
Anthony Kastor
Ann Kaufman
Mary Kellett
Michael Kelso
Jihyon Kim
George Kimmerle
Robert King
May Kirk
Bruno Kleimanis
Allen Klein
Francis Klein
Daniel Kocieniewski
Kay Kollar
Thomas Koloski
Eric Kopelson
Carla Kramer
Herbert Kunzel
Jonathan Lanman
Taylor Lauden
Howard Lauritano
Rayford Law

Young Lee
Betty Lee
Mark Levine
Kristin Lewis
Pamela Lloyd
Peter Lofgren
Harry Lyew
Peter Marino
David Marmor
Anton Martinez
Ana Marton
Lois Mate
Ted Matheny
Michael McCaffrey
Kevin McClurkan
James McCullar
Alice McGown
Brian McGrath
Martha McKee
Sherry McKibben
Shauna McManus
Alfred Medioli
Peter Medure
Ezra Mersey
Richard Metzner
Carol Meyer
Lynn Michaels
Blake Middleton
Townsend Moore
Patricia Morton
Tadashi Murai
Thomas Myers
Richard Nadler
David Nahon
Timothy Nanni
Craig Nealy
Dorothy Neilson
Natalie Newey
Jennifer Nobis
Yugi Noga
Lisa Odyniec
George O'Shaughnessy
Hisayoshi Ota
Greg Palestri
Adrian Panaitescu
Clement Paulsen
Ann Pendleton
Mary Pepchinski
Steven Peppas
Dean Perton
Eric Peterson
Charmian Place
Ellyn Polshek
Peter Polshek
Jorge Porto
Elisabeth Post
Cricket Purdy
George Queral
Damu Radheshwar
Laurel Reich
Lisa Reindorf
James Rich
Terence Riley
Elizabeth Riordon
Mark Robbins
Susan Rodriguez

Victor Rodriguez
Holly Ross
Annette Rusin
James Russell
Mark Rylander
Barbara Sageser
Eva Sandberg
Simona Scarlat
George Schieferdecker
Joel Schiffer
Elliot Jon Schrank
Sean Sculley
Robert Seitz
Carolyn Senft
Robert Sherry
Sassoon Shamoon
David Sherman
Marianne Shin
Edward Siegel
Gaston Silva
James Sinks
Joanne Sliker
Shawn Slutsky
Vicki Smith
Catherine Snodgrass
Karen Sobol
Michael Starr
Susanna Steeneken
Jeanne Stinnett
Eugene Stueben
Howard Sussel
Peter Sweeny
Hans Tak
Peter Talbot
Dwight Talley
Peter Tao
Tapani Tapanainen
Leslie Thomas
Richard Thompson
Frank Thristino
Gerd Thurstac
Marian Tlush
Richard Tobin
David Tobin
Lisa Tolman
Neil Troiano
Dale Turner
Francis Turner
Louis Turpin
Dimitris Varangis
Ronald Vargo
Thomas Viani
Margaret Walker
Donna Wax
John Weick
Don Weinreich
David Westover
Alan Willig
Sarah Willmer
Ann Wimsatt
Charles Wolf
Michael Woods
James Wright
Barry Yanku
Larry Young
Daniel Zito

Photograph Credits

Illustrations copyright © the following.

Peter Aaron/ESTO: p.44, top left; p.48, right; p.174, 6,8; p.175, 9; p.237, 3; p.238, 4; p.239, 6.

Gil Amiaga: p.29, bottom left; p.30, bottom left; p.35, bottom right; p.36, bottom left, top right; p.37, top left, bottom right; p.42, top right; p.43, left; p.64, 1,2; p.65, 1,2; p.99, 3,4; p.164, 1; p.170, 1; p.171, 1; p.214, 2,3,4,5.

Patricia Layman Bazelon: p.48, left; p.191, 4.

Robert Beckhard: p.27, top right; p.28, center left; p.29, top left, top right, bottom right; p.31, top left; p.37, bottom left; p.41, top left; p.76, 4; p.77, 5,6,7,8; p.84, 1; p.85, 4; p.81, 2; p.146, 1; p.147, 1; p.148, 2; p.149, 5,6; p.204, 1; p.205, 3; p.215, 1; p.236, 2,5,7.

Byron Bell: p.71, 6.

Serge Bluds: p.30, top right.

Robert L. Bracklow, circa 1900: p.106, 4.

Van Brody: p.78, 1,2; p.79, 3; p.127, 1,2.

Langdon Clay: p.56, right; p.246, 2; p.247, 3; p.71, 11; p.99, 8; p.99, 7.

Dan Cornish/ESTO: p.143, 4.

George Cserna: p.30, center left, center right; p.31, bottom left, right; p.32, left, bottom right; p.110, 5,6; p.111, 7; p.112, 1; p.123, 4,5; p.151, 2; p.152, 6,7; p.166, 1; p.167, 2,3; p.169, 8; p.206, 1; p.207, 2; p.228, 1; p.229, 2.

Davis, Brody & Associates: p.71, 8.

David Franzen/ESTO: p.40, right; p.156, 2,4; p.157, 6,7.

Jeff Goldberg/ESTO: p.147, 7; p.180, 5; p.181, 6.

Jim Horner: p.56, top left; p.116, 3; p.50, bottom left.

Wolfgang Hoyt/ESTO: p.71, 12.

Timothy Hursley: p.112, 2.

Kallmann, McKinnell & Wood, Architects, Inc.: p.71, 9.

Elliott Kaufman: p.99, 6,9; p.98, 1,2.

Kawasumi Architectural Photographic Office: p.26, center left, bottom left; p.197, 3; p.198, 6,7; p.199, 10.

Fred Knubel: p.34, left.

Balthazar Korab: p.102, 5,6; p.103, 7,8; p.150, 1.

Nathaniel Lieberman: p.31 center left; p.57, right; p.118, 2; p.153, 1; p.154, 4,5; p.155, 6; p.168, 4.

Norman McGrath: p.71, 10,13; p.41, bottom left; p.234, 1; p.235, 3,4,5,6.

Duane Michals: p.248.

Andrew Moore: p.47, top right; p.218, 5.

Osamu Murai: p.201, 5,6; p.202, 8,9,10.

Richard Payne: p.71, 3.

Burns Photographic, Inc.: p.109, 4.

James Stewart Polshek, p.144, 10.

Jock Pottle: p.71, 1.

Stan Ries: p.177.

Cervin Robinson: p.71, 4; p.85, 6; p.90, 5,7; p.91, 8; p.43 right.

Laura Rosen: p.35, top right, center right; p.37, top right; p.41, center left, bottom right; p.42, top left, center left, bottom left; p.44, top left; p.80, 1; p.82, 5; p.84, 2; p.93, 11,13; p.94, 15,17,18; p.96, 1; p.130, 7; p.212, 1; p.213, 3; p.232, 1; p.233; p.239, 1.

John Schupf: p.245, 4.

Robert A.M. Stern/Edmund Stoecklein: p.71, 7.

Edmund Stoecklein: p.33, top left; p.36, bottom right; p.38, left; p.124, 1; p.125, 3; p.126, 6,7; p.210, 1; p.211, 3,4; p.230, 1; p.231, 3,4,5,6.

Ezra Stoller/ESTO: p.74, 3,4; p.75, 1.

Alan Stuart: p. 114, 5.

Studio New York Times: p.25, right; p.26, top left.

Y. Takase, Retoria, Y Futagawa & Associated Photographer: p.58, bottom left; p.190, 2.

Paul Warchol: p.44, center left; p.52, top left; p.47, bottom right; p.41, top right; p.71, 5; p.86, 1; p.87, 3,4; p.95, 20; p.115, 7; p.131, 8; p.176, 1; p.178, 2,3; p.179, 4; p.241 3,4; p.242, 1; p.243, 3,4,5.

Illustrations reprinted courtesy of the following:
p.21, left: *George Howe: Toward A Modern Architecture*, Robert A.M. Stern (New Haven, Conn.: Yale University Press, 1975); p. 21, top right: Mrs. Leone Nalle; p. 21, bottom right: *Painting Toward Architecture* (New York: Duell, Sloan, Pierce, 1948), p. 59; p. 22, right: *Louis I. Kahn: L'uomo, il maestro*, Alessandra Latour, ed. (Rome: Edizioni Kappa, 1986); p. 22, left: *Katsura Villa*, text by Arata Isozaki, photographs by Yashiro Ishimoto (Tokyo: Iwanami Shoten, Publishers, 1983), p. 214; p. 23, left: *Erich Mendelsohn*, Bruno Zevi (New York: Rizzoli International Publications, 1985), p. 53; p. 60, 1; *Modern Architecture*, Manfredo Tafuri and Francesco Dal Co (New York: Harry N. Abrams, Inc., 1979), p. 46; p. 60, 2: *Paris: A Century of Change 1878–1978* Norma Evenson (New Haven, Conn.: Yale University Press, 1979), p. 16; p. 60, 3: *Architecture: From Pre-History to Post-Modernism*, Marvin Trachtenberg and Isabel Hyman (Englewood Cliffs, N.J.: Prentice-Hall, Inc., p. 555); p. 60, 4: *Design in America: The Cranbrook Vision 1925– 1950* (New York: Harry N. Abrams, Inc, with the Detroit Institute of the Arts and the Metropolitan Museum of Art, 1983), p. 53; p. 71, 14: *James Stirling: Buildings and Projects*, Peter Arnell and Ted Bickford, eds. (New York: Rizzoli International Publications, 1984); p. 72, 1: *Architecture: From Pre-History to Post-Modernism*, p. 21; p. 72, 2: *Egyptian Architecture*, Jean-Louis De Ceneval (New York: Grosset & Dunlap, 1964), p. 78; p. 106,1: *James Stirling: Buildings and Projects*, p. 178; p. 106, 3: *Erich Mendelsohn*, p. 54; p. 120, 1: *Architecture: From Pre-History to Post-Modernism*, p. 123; p. 120, 3: *Architecture: From Pre-History to Post-Modernism*, p. 450; p. 144, 3: *Great Architecture of the World*, John Julius Norwich, ed. (New York: Random House, Inc., in association with American Heritage Publishing Co., Inc., 1975), p. 158; p. 162, 2: *Perspecta 21: The Yale Architecture Journal* (Cambridge, Mass.: MIT Press, 1984), p. 21; p. 192, 4: *Architecture: From Pre-History to Post-Modernism*, p. 535; p. 226, 1: *L'Architecture de l'Art Nouveau*, Frank Russell (Paris: Berger-Levrault Publishers, 1982), p. 46; p. 226, 2: *Pierre Chareau*, Marc Vellay and Kenneth Frampton (Paris: Editions du Regard, 1984), p. 276; p. 226, 3: *Architecture: From Pre-History to Post-Modernism*, p. 428; p. 226, 4: *Carlo Scarpa, Opera Completa*, Francesco Dal Co and Giuseppe Mazzariol (Milan: Electa, 1984), p. 65.

DATE DUE
